Teacher's Resource Book

Diana Anyakwo

With Caroline Nixon and Michael Tomlinson

Contents

0	Introduction	Page 4
1	A song and a dance	Page 6
2	Big wide world	Page 15
3	Shopping around	Page 24
4	Getting about	Page 33
5	Study smarter	Page 42
6	Good job!	Page 51
7	It's the law!	Page 60
8	Fantastic flavours	Page 69
9	Raining cats and dogs!	Page 78

Introduction

This Teacher's Resource Bank is designed to help you and your learners make the most of *Power Up* Level 6. There are seven photocopiable worksheets for each unit, as well as teaching notes.

What do the photocopiable worksheets provide?

The worksheets have been carefully designed to reinforce and provide extra practice of the language and skills taught through the Pupil's Book and Activity Book.

Each worksheet has accompanying teaching notes with suggestions for exploitation in the classroom, along with answer keys and audioscripts. The teaching notes also include optional follow-up tasks, which are suitable for providing either extra support or extra challenge.

Vocabulary practice worksheets

There are two Vocabulary worksheets per unit. These worksheets reinforce each of the two new lexical sets taught in the unit. The activities in these worksheets focus on both the recognition of the new words, as well as the ability to write the new words with minimal support. Activities in the Vocabulary worksheets are varied and fun and using them also helps learners to develop other skills, such as fine motor skills, categorising, sequencing and drawing.

Grammar practice worksheets

There are two worksheets per unit which focus on the two main grammar points presented in each unit. In these worksheets, activities use known vocabulary with the new grammar point and provide practice in the context of the unit topic. Activities include writing answers, reordering sentences and describing differences. You can use the worksheets with learners who finish classwork quickly. Alternatively, you can use them with learners who need further reinforcement of a particular grammar point.

Skills worksheets

There are also two Skills worksheets per unit. These are a Listening and speaking worksheet and a Reading and writing worksheet. In this way, there is a balance between productive and receptive skills in each unit. The worksheets focus on language from that particular unit, but they also recycle language from earlier units. The pairs of worksheets in each unit are linked by their topic, which helps increase learner confidence and motivation.

The Listening and speaking worksheets exploit situations which are relevant to the age group, such as listening to students talking about a school trip, or talking about clothes and sports. The listening activities are to be used with the whole class. There are a variety of listening activities, all of which are practised in the Pupil's Book and Activity Book, and which echo the Cambridge Key or Preliminary exam tasks. Speaking activities usually have some kind of guessing or describing element and require learners to work in pairs or groups to share information and voice their own opinions. The teaching notes support you in setting up these tasks.

The Reading and writing worksheets can be used individually or as a whole class. Reading tasks are varied and are designed to be similar to the task types in the Cambridge Key or Preliminary exams. The reading tasks also provide an opportunity to look at traditions and practices from other countries in some detail, while still being linked to the unit topic. The writing tasks encourage the learners to write a short text of their own, which is usually in the form of a personal reaction to the cultural information in the reading text, or asks the learners to make comparisons between the new culture and their own. This writing output is always supported in the form of first asking learners to work in a group to discuss and make notes on the topic, prompted by the questions on the worksheet.

Mission worksheets

There are nine worksheets for the Mission sections, so one per unit. Each Mission, or project, has been broken down into three different stages, occurring at different points in the unit. The Mission worksheets support one or more of these stages, depending on what is needed. They provide some kind of output task which contributes to the whole project. Generally these activities have a communicative focus and work will be carried out in either pairs or groups, and will require some teacher input. See the Teacher's Book Introduction for further information on the Missions.

How can the worksheets be used?

You can use the Vocabulary and Grammar worksheets with individuals who complete their work in class quickly. Alternatively, you can set these worksheets for homework, or use them with learners who would benefit from some extra practice. However, the Listening and speaking and Reading and writing worksheets need to be used in small groups and pairs, and can be used when additional practice is necessary. Or, they can provide you with an alternative when there is a change or gap in your usual routine.

Learner portfolios

The worksheets also lend themselves to being compiled and stored so that learners have a record of their work for the year and they can see the progress they have made and reflect on the work they have done. Compiling a portfolio can develop learner autonomy and is a good way to increase parent involvement, since it can be shared with family and friends. Portfolios are also useful for you as a teacher because they are something tangible to show parents at the end of a term or year.

Learners can either stick the worksheets into a scrapbook or notebook, or keep them in a file or ring binder. A useful alternative is an electronic copy of the worksheets, where learners scan their worksheets and store them on a hard drive or cloud. Not only do learners have something that they are more likely to keep, but also they can develop IT skills at the same time.

1 A song and a dance

Vocabulary 1

Using the worksheet

- This worksheet provides practice of the core words: *disco, folk, jazz, hip-hop, classical music, opera, studio, recording, stage*.

1 Learners work individually to look at the pictures and find the music words in the wordsearch. They then write the words under the corresponding picture.

> Key: 1 hip-hop, 2 jazz, 3 stage, 4 recording, 5 studio, 6 folk, 7 disco, 8 opera

2 Learners read the text and unscramble the words. Fast finishers can make a mind map of the new vocabulary in their notebooks.

> Key: 1 hip-hop, 2 folk, 3 jazz, 4 classical music, 5 disco, 6 pop

Optional follow-up activity (extension):

Play 'Minute Race'. Ask learners to sit in a circle. Set a timer (such as the one on your phone) for one minute. Say music words. Learners take turns calling out the vocabulary items around the circle. They have to get around the whole circle before the minute is up. If you have a large class, you could ask learners to say as many words as they can in one minute.

Grammar 1

Using the worksheet

- This worksheet provides practice of the target language of adjectives with prepositions: *for, to, about, at, on, with*.

1 Learners work individually. They read the text and circle the correct answers. Then learners write the adjectives and prepositions in their notebooks.

> Key: 1 for, 2 about, 3 with, 4 at, 5 on

2 Learners work in pairs. They look at the pictures and write complete sentences with the expressions in the box.

> Example answers:
> 1 I am worried about the weather.
> 2 I am good at playing the cello.
> 3 I am proud of the concert.
> 4 I am excited about my birthday.
> 5 I am bored with the TV.

3 Learners work in pairs to play the card game. They cut out each set of cards, then place them face down in two piles. Learners take turns to pick a card from each pile and make a sentence about themselves with the adjective and preposition written on the card. Their partner decides if the sentence is correct. Monitor pairs and check they are reading out the correct sentences. If they make a correct sentence, they keep the cards. If the adjective/preposition combination doesn't work, they put the cards back into the pile, shuffle them and pick up another pair. At the end of the game, learners will have some non-matching adjectives/preposition pairs. Ask learners to lay them out on the table and take turns to make sentences.

Optional follow-up activity (reinforcement):

Write the following on the board: *Something you're ... afraid of, bored with, excited about, pleased with, proud of, worried about, good at*. Ask learners to read the prompts and think of one or two words for each one. As an example, write your list on the board (in no particular order): *concert, spiders, art project, book, music, exam*. Ask a confident learner to ask you about your list, e.g. *I think you are proud of the concert. No, I'm proud of my art project*. Learners then continue playing with the remaining adjectives and guessing which activity or thing they match.

Vocabulary 2

Using the worksheet

- This worksheet provides practice of the core adjectives: *patient, charming, reliable, bossy, rude, cheerful, generous, serious, intelligent*.

1 Learners match the two parts of the sentences. Fast finishers can write the words and definitions in their notebooks.

> Key: 1 c, 2 g, 3 e, 4 b, 5 f, 6 h, 7 i, 8 d, 9 a

2 Learners read and complete the text with the correct words.

> Key: 1 reliable, 2 cheerful, 3 patient, 4 bossy, 5 rude

Optional follow-up activity (extension):

Play an oral word association game. You need a small ball or beanbag. Throw the ball to a learner and call out one of the core adjectives. The learner with the ball or beanbag says a word linked to the adjective (quickly and without needing to explain the link) and throws the ball to another learner. The next learner says a word linked to the previous word, and so on. If time allows, you could write up the word association chains as the learners play and then go over them at the end of each chain.

Grammar 2

Using the worksheet

- This worksheet provides practice of the target language *so/nor* with auxiliaries.

1 Learners work individually to correct the sentences. Then learners write the complete corrected sentences in their notebooks.

> Key: 1 (do) did, 2 (did) do, 3 (do) have, 4 (have) would, 5 (is) am, 6 (am) did

2 Learners read and complete the dialogue. Fast finishers can work in pairs to role play the dialogue. Invite some pairs to role play for the class.

> Key: 1 have, 2 do, 3 did, 4 would, 5 do

3 Learners work in pairs. They use the words in the box to talk about things they like/don't like using so/nor + auxiliaries. You could ask some pairs to share their ideas with the class.

Optional follow-up activity (reinforcement):

Learners work in pairs. Ask them to think of three more things they like/don't like and then and write a three short dialogues using the target grammar so/nor + auxiliary. Monitor and check role plays. Learners can then role play their dialogues for the class.

Skills 1: Listening and speaking

Using the worksheet

- This worksheet provides listening and speaking skills practice talking about music. The listening skill is listening for specific information.

1 Play the audio for learners to listen. Ask a gist question to check understanding of the audio, e.g. *What are Lucy and Adam deciding?* What each of the team members will write about.

> Key: 1 D, 2 G, 3 F, 4 B, 5 C

Track 01

Adam: I'm really excited about our music project.
Lucy: So am I.
Adam: I think we should plan what we are going to do for the music project.
Lucy: So do I.
Adam: Each of us can write about a different type of music.
Lucy: Good idea.
Adam: Karen loves folk music so she could write about that.
Lucy: So does Cathy. They could both work on that together.
Adam: Good. Peter can write about jazz; he loves that. I don't like it.
Lucy: Nor do I. I'd like to learn more about classical music.
Adam: So would I. I would be happy to write about hip-hop and you could do classical music.
Lucy: I'm happy with that. I could also write something about opera.
Adam: Great. I'll write about Jay-Z. He's famous for his hip-hop music. What about disco? James loved the disco music concert last weekend.
Lucy: So did I. It was a great concert.
Adam: James can write about disco.
Lucy: What about pop? Are we going to include that in the project?
Adam: No, I don't think we should.
Lucy: OK then. I think we've got everything organised!

2 Learners work in pairs and discuss the pictures.

3 Learners ask and answer the questions. Ask pairs to share their ideas with the class.

Optional follow-up activity (extension):

Ask learners to practice listening for specific information. Choose some words from the dialogue, e.g. *jazz, hip-hop, folk, classical music, opera, pop, disco, concert*. Add a few distractor words, e.g. *studio, recording, rock, rap*. Write the words on the board. Explain to learners that you are going to play the audio, and when they hear one of the words they should stand up or put up their hand.

Skills 2: Reading and writing

Using the worksheet

- This worksheet provides reading and writing skills practice in understanding a text about music from around the world. The text is about different types of music found in Korea, Britain and Cuba.

1 Learners read the texts. Ask learners what they think of the texts. Have they heard of any of the different types of music? Which would they like to listen to?

> Key: 1 A, 2 B, 3 A, 4 C, 5 C, 6 A, 7 B

2 Learners research online a musical genre found in their country. They can print out pictures and stick them next to their sentences.

3 Learners work in pairs and compare the music in their country with the music mentioned in the texts.

Optional follow-up activity (extension):

Learners research another type of music from another country online. They can print pictures and write three or four sentences. They can then share their text with their partner. Learners with smartphones can find and play a sample of the music for their partner.

7

Vocabulary 1

1 Look and find the different types of music words in the puzzle. Write the words under the pictures.

R	E	R	H	I	P	H	O	P
A	E	D	F	G	H	J	K	M
S	Z	C	F	C	S	V	B	N
Q	W	E	O	R	T	Y	U	
Z	A	S	L	R	U	D	F	H
X	K	O	K	D	D	J	R	S
C	G	S	G	L	I	I	E	T
V	D	I	S	C	O	K	N	A
B	J	A	Z	Z	D	I	W	G
N	S	D	N	O	B	Y	B	E

2 Look and unscramble the words.

Blog

Last year I went to a music festival in England. It was fantastic. There was lots of different types of music. Some of my favourite musicians and bands performed. Tiny Tempah and Jay Z were there. They rapped and performed **(1)** *phopih* _____ songs. There was a **(2)** *olkf* _____ band called Mumford & Sons that I really liked. They played English folk music. There was also a **(3)** *azjz* _____ band from America. They were cool. I was really surprised that there was also **(4)** *lacislasc smcui* _____ at the festival. They played Beethoven. I really enjoyed it. The best band was on Saturday night – it was Chic and Nile Rodgers – they played **(5)** *cdosi* _____ music.

⭐ 1 Grammar 1

1 **Circle the correct words to complete the text.**

4Square are an exciting new folk band. They are famous **(1)** *for/to* their beautiful songs. They are very excited **(2)** *for/about* their first world tour. They are starting out in London and then travelling to 20 cities around the world. Their fans are pleased **(3)** *for/with* their new album. The band is good **(4)** *about/at* mixing traditional folk songs with new pop songs to create their own unique style. If you are keen **(5)** *on/at* discovering new music, then check out this fantastic new band.

2 **Look at the expressions in the box and complete the sentences so they are correct for you.**

> excited about   worried about   good at   proud of   bored with

1 I am _____
2 I am _____
3 I am _____
4 I am _____
5 I am _____

3 **Cut out the adjectives and prepositions. Use the cards to make sentences about you.**

Instructions
Cut out the preposition and adjective cards and place them face down in two piles.
Each learner takes a turn to pick up a preposition and adjective card and makes a sentence.

in	about	or	at	to	with
on	of	for	about	in	of

famous	interested	proud	keen	afraid	bored
pleased	happy	similar	tired	excited	good

I'm interested in opera.   *I'm afraid of spiders.*

Vocabulary 2

1 Match the two parts of the sentences.

1 Alexis is a cheerful person,   a she always interrupts you.
2 David is reliable,   b he is always telling people what to do.
3 Julie is serious,   c she is always positive.
4 Karl is bossy,   d she gives things to others.
5 Henry is charming,   e she doesn't laugh often.
6 Emma is intelligent,   f he gets on with everyone.
7 Toby is patient,   g he has never missed work.
8 Amy is generous,   h she always gets answers right.
9 Kelly is rude,   i he doesn't get angry when he has to wait.

2 Read and complete the text with the correct words from Activity 1.

Community Noticeboard

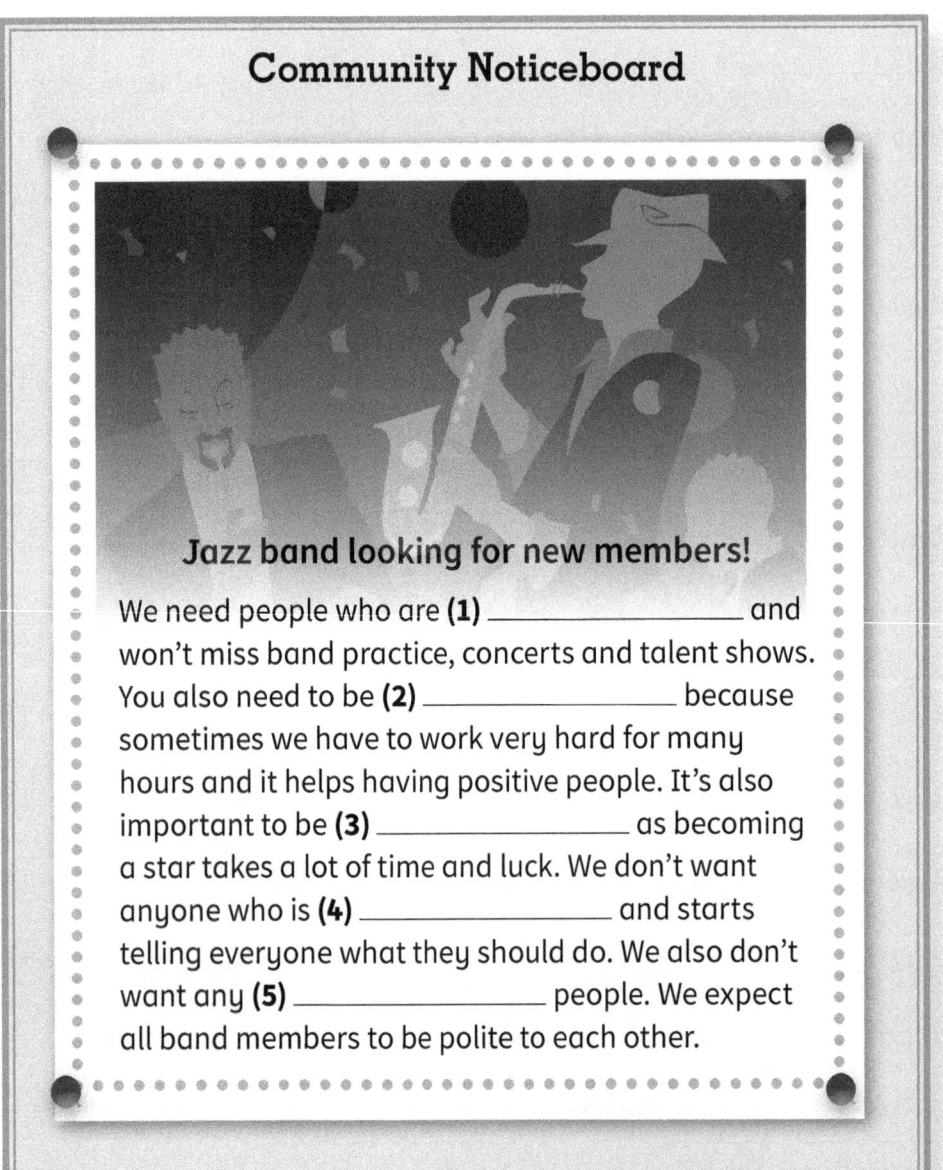

Jazz band looking for new members!

We need people who are **(1)** _____ and won't miss band practice, concerts and talent shows. You also need to be **(2)** _____ because sometimes we have to work very hard for many hours and it helps having positive people. It's also important to be **(3)** _____ as becoming a star takes a lot of time and luck. We don't want anyone who is **(4)** _____ and starts telling everyone what they should do. We also don't want any **(5)** _____ people. We expect all band members to be polite to each other.

Grammar 2

1 Find and correct the mistakes in the sentences. Write the correct sentences on the lines.

1 I enjoyed the concert. So do I. _____
2 Maria doesn't like classical music. Neither did I. _____
3 I've never seen a jazz concert. Nor do I. _____
4 I'd like to go to a hip-hop concert. So have I. _____
5 I'm not rude. Neither is I. _____
6 John went to the classical music concert. So am I. _____

2 Read and complete the dialogue with the correct words from the box.

do   would   did   have   do

Paula: Hey, Peter. What are you looking at?
Peter: It's a website about opera.
Paula: Really? I've never been to an opera.
Peter: Neither **(1)** _____ I.
Paula: I like classical music.
Peter: So **(2)** _____ I.
Paula: There was a classical music concert in the park last week but I didn't go.
Peter: Neither **(3)** _____ I.
I was at football practice.
Paula: I'd like to go to the opera.
Peter: So **(4)** _____ I.
Shall we go to this one? I think it looks interesting.
Paula: So **(5)** _____ I.
Yes, let's get the tickets.

3 Work with a partner. Use the ideas in the box, *so/nor* plus an auxiliary verb to talk about things you like/don't like.

hip-hop   folk   jazz   classical   pop   rock   disco   opera

I like jazz music.   So do I.

# Skills 1: Listening and speaking

1  You will hear Adam talking to Lucy about a music project. What type of music does each person like? Draw a line from the name to the type of music.

People	Music
Cathy	pop
Peter	classical
Adam	disco
Lucy	folk
James	rock
	hip-hop
	jazz

2 Work with a partner. Look at the pictures. Say what type of music you think is shown in each. Which do you like?

3 Work in pairs. Ask and answer the questions.

1 What kind of music do you usually listen to? Why do you like it?
2 How does it make you feel?
3 What kind of music don't you like? Why?
4 Do you enjoy going to concerts? Why? Why not?
5 Why do you think people listen to music?

# Skills 2: Reading and writing

 Read the text about different music from around the world.

K pop
K-pop is a type of music that comes from South Korea. It is a mixture of pop, rap, **hip-hop** and rock. It started in 1996 when the first K-pop band – H.O.T. released their first song. Today one of the most popular K-pop groups are Psy. He is **famous for** his song 'Gangnam Style'. It had over 3.1 billion YouTube views!

British folk
The folk music of England is a traditional type of music. People in the UK have been **keen on** folk for hundreds of years. The modern version started developing in the 19th and 20th centuries. The music combines traditional styles with modern rock, pop and even **classical music**. Ed Sheeran is a famous British singer who sings folk. Mumford & Sons are another popular band.

Afro-Cuban jazz
Afro-Cuban **jazz** is a music style from Cuba. It is a mix of traditional jazz and African drums. Musicians developed the style in Cuba in the 1940s and 50s. Mario Bauza is **known for** bringing Afro-Cuban jazz to a larger audience. A well-known musician from that time was Tito Puente. He created beautiful songs that people were **excited about** because they could dance to them. Today The Carlos Adames Group and Jose Cornier are popular Afro-Cuban jazz musicians.

Which type of music …

		K-pop	Folk	Afro-Cuban Jazz
1	is from Korea?	A	B	C
2	has been around for hundreds of years?	A	B	C
3	does Psy make?	A	B	C
4	uses African drumming styles?	A	B	C
5	started in the 1940s and 50s?	A	B	C
6	started in 1996?	A	B	C

2 Think about a type of music from your country. Make notes in your notebook.
1 What is it called?
2 When did it start?
3 What kind of music is it?
4 Who are some popular musicians and bands?

3 Choose one of the types of music from Activity 1. What is the same/what is different from music from your country?

_____

_____

_____

PHOTOCOPIABLE   Power Up TRB 6 © Cambridge University Press and UCLES 2018

Mission Stage 1: A concert review

1 Make a list of your favourite types of music. Which band or singer would you like to see in concert? Why?

	Types of music
1	
2	
3	
4	
5	
6	

I would like to see _____ in concert because _____
_____
_____
_____
_____

2 Write a review of a concert you have been to. If you haven't been to one, you can make up an imaginary experience.

2 Big wide world

Vocabulary 1
Using the worksheet
- This worksheet provides practice of the core words: *Africa, Antarctica, Asia, Australia, Europe, North America, South America, nationalities, languages, climate, culture, landscapes.*

1 Learners work individually. They use the clues to complete the puzzle.

> Key: **Across** 1 Africa 3 Europe 5 North America 6 Antarctica 7 Asia **Down** 2 Australia 4 South America

2 Learners can work in pairs. They read the sentences and decide if the words in bold are used correctly or incorrectly. If they are incorrect, they write the correct words on the lines.

> Key: 1 ✗ languages 2 ✗ climates, 3 ✓ 4 ✗ landscapes 5 ✓

3 Learners work in pairs to play the game. They take turns to think of a continent and say the first letter. Their partner has to guess which continent it is. They can ask up to three questions.

Optional follow-up activity (extension):
Play 'Draw it'. Divide learners into two teams. Invite one or two members from each team in turn to the front and whisper a word from the vocabulary set to them. The team members have to draw a clue for their team to guess the word.

Grammar 1
Using the worksheet
- This worksheet provides practice of the target language of adjectives with prepositions.

1 Learners work individually. They read the text and circle the correct answers.

> Key: 1 a, c, 2 b, 3 b, 4 b, 5 a, 6 c

2 Learners work in pairs. They read the sentences and decide if they are defining or non-defining. They add commas to the sentences where necessary.

> Key: 1 D, 2 D, 3 ND Maria, who is from Australia, can speak three languages. 4 D, 5 ND Mali, which is a country in Africa, has got a very hot climate. 6 D

3 Learners work in pairs. They look at the pictures and complete the sentences with their own ideas. Ask pairs to share their ideas with the class.

> Key: Suggested answers:
> 1 William Shakespeare is the writer who wrote *Macbeth*.
> 2 The Eiffel Tower is a monument which is in Paris.
> 3 Mount Everest is the mountain that many people try to climb.
> 4 Leonardo da Vinci is the artist who painted the Mona Lisa.
> 5 Fara is a student whose mum is a teacher.

Optional follow-up activity (reinforcement):
Learners play a sentence building game. Divide them into groups of three or four. Write a list of famous places or monuments, e.g. *The Amazon, The Statue of Liberty, Australia, The Louvre, Antarctica.* Ask each group to choose one of the places and say something true about the place, e.g. *The Amazon is in South America.* The next learner has to repeat what the first learner said but add some extra information, e.g. *The Amazon, which is a river, is in South America.* The next learner tries to expand the sentence, e.g. *The Amazon, which is a river that is the longest in the world, is in South America.* Continue until a learner makes a factual mistake or gives up.

Vocabulary 2
Using the worksheet
- This worksheet provides practice of the core vocabulary: *canal, campsite, tent, cliffs, valley, seaside, bay, port, scenery.*

1 Learners work in pairs. They use the code to complete the sentences. Fast finishers can write new sentences in their notebooks with the words.

> Key: 1 canal, 2 campsite, 3 tent, 4 cliffs, 5 valley, 6 seaside

2 Learners look at the pictures and read the text. You could elicit the pictures before they read the text. They then complete the missing words.

> Key: 1 scenery, 2 valleys, 3 port, 4 bay, 5 campsite, 6 tent

Optional follow-up activity (extension):
Play 'Minute Race'. Ask learners to sit in a circle. Set a timer for one minute. You can use a timer on your phone. Say: *words for places around us*, e.g. *seaside.* Learners take turns calling out the vocabulary items. They have to get around the circle before the minute is up.

15

Grammar 2

Using the worksheet

- This worksheet provides practice of the target language: *more than..., fewer than... less than..., the most, the fewest, the least*.

1 Learners work individually and reorder the sentences.

> Key: Suggested answers:
> 1 Cars are less popular than bicycles in Amsterdam.
> 2 There are more than eight campsites in this area.
> 3 Our canal boat trip around England took fewer than 20 days.
> 4 Antarctica is the continent with the fewest people living on it.
> 5 Death Valley has the least rainy climate in North America.

2 Learners complete the text with the correct words.

> Key: 1 least, 2 most, 3 than, 4 the, 5 fewer

3 Learners work in pairs to look at the pictures and complete the sentences with their own ideas.

Optional follow-up activity (reinforcement):

Divide the class into groups of three or four. Each group has to write four sentences about the people in their class using the target grammar, e.g. *more than..., fewer than... less than ..., the most, the fewest, the least*. You could write an example sentence on the board, e.g. *Maria uses the bus less than Juan*. When they finish, groups can read out their sentences and the learners can confirm if they are true or not. Walk around the class and read them.

Skills 1: Listening and speaking

Using the worksheet

- This worksheet provides listening and speaking skills practice talking about a geography project. The listening skill is listening for gist.

1 Play the audio. Ask gist questions, e.g. 1 *What are the friends talking about?* Their project 2 *What lesson are the learners in?* Geography 3 *Where are the friends?* In the countryside.

> Key: 1 C, 2 B, 3 C, 4 B, 5 C

Track 02

Rachel: Mark, shall we start planning the geography project?
Mark: What **continent** shall we write about?
Rachel: **Antarctica** is the continent **which** is **the most** interesting for me.
Mark: Yes, but I think Frank and Jessica are doing that.
Rachel: **Africa**?
Mark: I wrote an essay about African **culture** last week.
Rachel: **South America**?
Mark: Good idea! It's the **continent** where the Amazon is. That will be really interesting!
Teacher: OK. I've written the continents on the board. We studied them and learnt some facts about them last week. I'd like you to choose one and draw its map. Then write facts about its **climate**, **culture**, **languages** and **landscape**. Don't use the Internet or any books. Please switch off your phones. Try to remember what you learnt. Try to include **more than** three facts.

Adam: That's the **valley where** we saw the horses.
Molly: I think if we keep walking on this path we will come to the **cliffs**.
Adam: Look at that house. There's a girl playing outside. She's the girl **whose** mother is a famous writer.
Molly: Let's go and say hello.
Adam: On the way back we can stop at the **seaside** town **that** has lots of nice restaurants.
Molly: Good idea

Peter: What website are you looking at?
Jane: I'm reading about the continents. This is really interesting. Did you know Asia is **the most** populated continent on Earth?
Peter: No, I didn't.
Jane: Antarctica is **the least** populated. It's also the continent **which** has the coldest climate.
Peter: Why are you reading about the continents?
Jane: Because I failed my geography exam.
Peter: Ah. Well, I have some geography homework about continents so this is very helpful! I'm going to see if there are any useful books here.

Mum: The **scenery** here is beautiful.
Lucy: Shall we walk down to the **bay** and go for a swim?
Mum: Yes, let's do that.
Lucy: **Which** campsite are we staying at?
Mum: **The least** expensive one. It's next to the forest.
Lucy: I want to stay at the one on the beach. It costs **less than** the one in the **valley**.
Mum: I know but you need to bring your own **tent** to that one and we haven't got one.

2 Learners work in pairs and discuss the pictures.
3 Learners ask and answer the questions. Ask pairs to share their ideas with the class.

Optional follow-up activity (extension):

Learners practice their listening skills again. Play the audio again and ask: 1 *Why doesn't Frank want to write about Africa?* (He already wrote an essay about it) 2 *Which is the most populated continent on Earth?* (Asia) 3 *Where are they going to swim?* (In the bay)

Skills 2: Reading and writing

Using the worksheet

- This worksheet provides reading and writing skills practice in understanding a text is about a woman who has travelled around Asia for a year.

1 Learners read the texts. Ask learners what they think of the texts. Have they been to any of the countries mentioned? Which would they like to visit?

> Key: 1 b, 2 c, 3 c

2 Learners write about a place they have visited. They can use the Internet to research facts and print out pictures and stick them next to their sentences. Ask individuals to share their ideas with the class.

2 Vocabulary 1

1 Use the clues to complete the puzzle.

Across

1 Ghana and Senegal are on this continent.
3 There are 50 countries in this continent.
5 There are 23 countries in this continent.
6 This continent is in the South Pole.
7 India is in this continent.

Down

2 This continent is a country.
4 Brazil is in this continent.

2 Read the sentences. If the word in bold is used correctly, tick the sentence. If the word in bold is used incorrectly, write the correct word on the line.

1 People in Switzerland speak three **nationalities**; French, German and Italian. _____

2 The **languages** in Australia; there are hot and rainy areas, hot dry deserts and cooler mountain areas. _____

3 You can learn about North American **culture** at the Metropolitan Museum of Art. _____

4 One of North America's most beautiful **climates** is at Yellow Stone National Park, which has mountains, forests, lakes and volcanoes. _____

5 The **nationality** of a person tells you which country they come from. _____

3 Work in pairs to play the game. Think of a continent or country from Activity 1. Give your partner a clue. Your partner can then ask three questions and guess which continent it is.

- The weather can be very hot.
- How many countries are there?
- one
- Does it begin with the letter A?
- Yes
- It's Australia.

PHOTOCOPIABLE   Power Up TRB 6 © Cambridge University Press and UCLES 2018   17

2 ★ Grammar 1

1 Choose the correct words from the list to complete the fact file about Brazil. Some gaps have two possible answers.

Brazil is a country **(1)** _____ is in South America. People **(2)** _____ come from Brazil speak Portuguese, but there are over 150 different languages spoken in the country by the native people. Rio de Janiero is the city **(3)** _____ you can see Sugarloaf Mountain and the famous Copacabana beach. The Amazon River, **(4)** _____ is the longest river in the world, runs through Brazil. Brazil is the country **(5)** _____ about 60% of the Amazon Rainforest is found. Football is the most popular sport in Brazil. Neymar, **(6)** _____ nationality is Brazilian, is one of the best players in the world.

1	**a** that	**b** where	**c** which	4	**a** that	**b** which	**c** whose
2	**a** whose	**b** who	**c** that	5	**a** where	**b** which	**c** that
3	**a** that	**b** where	**c** which	6	**a** who	**b** that	**c** whose

2 Decide if the clauses are defining write (D) or non-defining write (ND). Add commas where necessary.

1 Jennifer Lawrence is an actor who comes from America. _____
2 Ella is the girl whose mum is a teacher at my school. _____
3 Maria who is from Australia can speak three languages. _____
4 I'm wearing the T-shirt you bought me for my birthday. _____
5 Mali which is a country in Africa has got a very hot climate. _____
6 Alex Burke wrote a book about the different cultures of people in Brazil. _____

3 Work with a partner. Complete the sentences with your own ideas. Use relative clauses.

1 William Shakespeare is the writer _____
2 The Eiffel Tower is a monument _____
3 Mount Everest is the mountain _____
4 Leonardo da Vinci is the artist _____
5 Fara is a student _____ mum _____

Vocabulary 2

1 Use the key to break the code and write the missing words.

A	B	C	D	E	F	G	H	I	J	K	L	M
!	$	&	^	?	>	#	%	568	984	-	<	/
N	O	P	Q	R	S	T	U	V	W	X	Y	Z
(	£	)	@	897	254	=	223	*	+	987	435	756

1   We went on a & ! (! < boat in Amsterdam. _____
2   We stayed at a & ! /) 254 568 = ? in France. _____
3   I slept in a = ? (= in a field. _____
4   We stood on the &< 568 > > 254 and looked at the sea. _____
5   There was a * ! < < ? 435 between the two mountains. _____
6   Torquay is a pretty 254 ? ! 254 568 ^ ? town in the south of England. _____

2 Use the pictures and the words in the box to complete the text.

> Bay   campsite   tent   valleys   port   scenery

Welcome to South Africa

South Africa is famous for its beautiful **(1)** _____.

There are **(2)** _____, beaches and lakes.

The capital Cape Town has got a big **(3)** _____.

There are some cliffs near Cape Town that people like to visit. South Africa has many pretty seaside towns.

Mossey **(4)** _____ is very popular with tourists because of its great beaches.

There are also several **(5)** _____ near the beach if you want to go camping.

If you are interested in seeing wildlife, you can go on safari and see elephants, giraffes, lions and lots more animals. You can sleep in a **(6)** _____ under the stars and listen to the sounds of the animals.

2 Grammar 2

1 Reorder the sentences.

1 Amsterdam. less Cars bicycles are than popular in
_____

2 eight more in than are There area. campsites this
_____

3 boat canal Our trip around took fewer 20 than days. England
_____

4 continent Antarctica fewest the people living it. on the is with
_____

5 least climate the rainy North America. in Death Valley has
_____

2 Complete the text with the correct words.

Canada is a country in North America. It is a country with many different climates and landscapes. It has very cold winters and quite hot summers. The **(1)** _____ cold place in Canada is Victoria in British Columbia. The average temperature here is much higher than in other parts of the country. The western part of the country has the **(2)** _____ lakes, mountains and forests. The tallest mountain in Canada is Mount Logan. More **(3)** _____ 36 million people live in Canada. Nunavut in the north has the **(4)** _____ number of people. This area includes the Arctic, which is in the North Pole. The people who live here are called The Inuit. They have lived there for hundreds of years. The climate in this part of the country is very cold and dry. It is a difficult place to live, and that's why there are **(5)** _____ people living there.

3 Work in pairs. Complete and the sentences with your own ideas. Then share with another pair.

1 Africa is the most _____
2 The climate in Antarctica is less warm than _____
3 Fewer people live in _____
4 My town has the fewest _____
5 More than ten students in my class _____

Skills 1: Listening and speaking

1 🎧 02 **Circle the correct answer for each question.**

1 You will hear two friends talking about their project. What do they decide to do?
   A a project about Africa
   B a project about Antarctica
   C a project about South America

2 You will hear a teacher talking to her students. What does the teacher want her class to do?
   A use the Internet for research
   B draw maps and write facts about a continent
   C Switch on their phones

3 You will hear two friends talking. Where will they arrive if they continue on the path?
   A the valley   B a seaside town
   C the cliffs

4 You will hear two friends talking. Why is Jane learning about the continents?
   A because they are interesting
   B because she failed her geography exam
   C because she has to do her geography homework

5 You will hear a mother talking to her daughter. Where are they staying tonight?
   A on the campsite on the beach
   B on the campsite in the valley
   C on the campsite next to the forest

2 Work with a partner. Look at the pictures. Say what you can see in each picture.

In this picture I can see a valley. *I can also see…*

3 Work in pairs. Ask and answer the questions.

1 Have you been to any of the places in the pictures? Which ones?
2 What do you like to do on holiday?
3 Who do you usually go on holiday with?
4 What places near your town would you recommend to visitors?
5 Why do you think people like to visit places with beautiful scenery?

2 Skills 2: Reading and writing

1 Read the interview and answer the questions.

Cat Bailey's new book Discovering Asia *is in shops. Our journalist Henry Reed interviewed her.*

Q: Why did you go travelling?

A: I was bored with my job. Manchester, **which is the city I live in**, is quite a wet and windy place and I was fed up of the weather. But to be honest, those weren't the reasons. It was because I saw an advert about India. It's a fascinating place **which** has lots of different **cultures**, **languages** and **landscapes**. It also has different climates – dry deserts in the west, hot rainforests in the south and the cold and windy region in the north.

Q: What other countries did you visit?

A: China, Japan, Indonesia and Thailand. I wanted to go to Vietnam because it's the country **that** I knew **the least** about, but I didn't have enough time.

Q: Which was your favourite place?

A: The place I enjoyed **the most** was Jiuzhaigou in China. It's a place **that** has amazing scenery with cliffs, mountains and valleys. There is a lake that changes colour during the day. What made it so special was that I was there with a group of friends **that** I had made.

Q: Which place did you like **the least**?

A: There was a storm in Thailand. I was staying at a **campsite which** was on the beach. A big wave washed away my **tent**. The local people were very helpful. That's not to say I didn't enjoy Thailand. It's a beautiful country **that** has a very interesting **culture**.

Q: What advice do you have for anyone thinking of doing the same trip as you?

A: Take **less luggage than you think you'll need**. Find out information about the **climate** and culture before you go. You don't need to learn the local **languages**, but being able to say even a couple of words will help.

1 Why did Cat decide to travel?
   A She was bored with her job
   B She saw an advert
   C She didn't like the weather in the UK

2 Why was the trip to Jiuzhaigou her favourite?
   A Because of the beautiful scenery
   B Because of the lake
   C Because she shared the experience with other people

3 What was challenging about Thailand?
   A The storm
   B The people
   C The culture

2 Think about an interesting place you have visited. Make notes in your notebook.

1 Where was it? _____
2 What was the climate like? _____
3 Describe the scenery. _____
4 What did you like the most about the place? _____

 # Mission Stages 1 and 2: An encyclopaedia entry

1 Choose a country you would like to visit and plan your research.

encyclopaedia entry

Country: _____

Nationality	Language
Climate	Culture
Landscape	Other

2 Write five amazing facts about the country you chose.

_____
_____
_____
_____

3 Shopping around

Vocabulary 1
Using the worksheet
- This worksheet provides practice of the core words: *bargain, prices, credit card, receipt, shop assistant, cash, change.*

1 Learners work in pairs. They look at the pictures and then cross out the letters to make the words.

> Key: bargain, credit card, receipt, shop assistant, cash, change Secret word: prices

2 Learners work individually. They read the text and complete the missing words. Fast finishers can make a mind map of all the words in their notebooks.

> Key: 1 shop assistant, 2 prices, 3 bargain, 4 credit card, 5 cash

Optional follow-up activity (extension):
Play 'Vocabulary Ladders'. Two teams stand at the board and write words in a column related to a given topic. Divide the class into two teams. Ask each team to stand in a line at the back of the classroom. Draw two columns and write Team A in the first and Team B in the second. Shout out the vocabulary topic and a member from each team has to race to the front and write a word related to that topic. This continues down the line until learners have written all the words. The first team to finish wins.

Grammar 1
Using the worksheet
This worksheet provides practice of the target language of verb + gerund and verb + infinitive. Divide learners into groups of three. Each group needs one worksheet. Ask learners to make counters from paper. Provide a dice for each group. Read the instructions for the game. Explain that learners have to use their own ideas. Demonstrate with the second square. Write the prompts on the board and elicit a sentence, i.e. I can't imagine moving to Antarctica. If a learner lands on a square a previous player has landed on they have to make up their own sentence using a gerund or infinitive form. If they land on a blank they make up a sentence. They can use the verbs in the boxes to help them or their own ideas. Learners play the game until the last player has reached the finish line.

Optional follow-up activity (extension):

> Key: 1 I can't imagine moving to Antarctica.
> 2 Helen doesn't mind helping me with my homework.
> 3 The shop owner plans to reduce the prices.
> 4 Blank square 5 We enjoy finding bargains in the sales. 6 I avoid carrying a lot of cash on me.
> 7 Tom agrees using credit cards to pay for things is convenient. 8 You won £100. Go forward three spaces and spend it! 9 He suggested going to the new department store. 10 She promised to clean the house.
> 11 You haven't got cash! Go back four spaces 12 Carol likes working as a shop assistant. 13 I prefer watching documentaries to dramas. 14 Blank square 15 I hate checking receipts. 16 Jessica plans to read the new Twilight book. 17 Blank square 18 I'd like to visit Rome. 19 He asked to watch TV. 20 You spent too much money with your credit card. Go back four places!
> 21 Blank square 22 I love reading books. 23 He'd like to be a footballer. 24 You have won £50. Go forward three! 26 I plan to visit my grand-parents in New York.
> 28 blank square 29 I can't imagine spending a lot of money on clothes. 30 Molly avoids going to the shops on Saturday because they are crowded.

Optional follow-up activity (reinforcement):
Write the following on the board: *promise, can't imagine, avoid, agree, suggest, enjoy, start, try, want, don't mind.* Divide learners into two teams. Give each team a set amount of time, e.g. Five minutes to write sentences with either the gerund or infinitive forms with the verbs from the board. The team to finish first wins.

Vocabulary 2
Using the worksheet
- This worksheet provides practice of the core vocabulary: *cost, return, selling, spend, exchange, a sale, for sale, reduced, second-hand, damaged, reasonable, luxury*

1 Learners match the parts of the words, then use the words to complete the sentences.

> Key: 1 second-hand, 2 reduced, 3 damaged, 4 luxury, 5 exchange, 6 spend, 7 sale, 8 selling

2 Learners read the text and complete the words. Fast finishers can write sentences with the vocabulary items in their notebooks.

> Key: 1 sale, 2 reasonable, 3 cost, 4 spend, 5 second-hand, 6 selling, 7 reduced

Optional follow-up activity (extension):
Play 'Relay Race'. Divide learners into teams of five and ask them to stand in lines. Give each player at the front a word, written on a piece of paper. The first player has to make up a sentence with the word and then pass it to

24

the person behind them. This player has to make up a different sentence with the word. When the word reaches the last person in the line they run to the front, say their sentence and place the word on the table. They can then take their place at the front of the line. The first team to finish are the winners.

Grammar 2
Using the worksheet
- This worksheet provides practice of the target language gerunds as subjects and objects.

1 Learners look at the pictures and complete the sentences with the correct gerund.

> Key: 1 shopping, 2 doing, 3 learning, 4 climbing, 5 playing

2 Learners complete the text with the correct gerunds.

> Key: 1 Shopping, 2 selling, 3 buying, 4 walking, 5 looking, 6 wearing

3 Learners complete the sentences individually then share their sentences with a partner.

Optional follow-up activity (reinforcement):
Draw a table with two columns. Write *team A* in the first column and *team B* in the second. Divide the class into two teams. Say *shopping* as a subject. Explain you want each team to write a sentence in which shopping is the subject. Nominated team members race to the board to write their sentence. The first to finish a correct sentence gains a point. Repeat with other gerunds and ask teams to write a sentence using the gerund as an object.

Skills 1: Listening and speaking
Using the worksheet
- This worksheet provides listening and speaking skills practice talking about shopping. The listening skill is listening for specific information

1 Play the audio. Ask gist questions to check understanding of the audio, e.g. 1 *Which kind of shop does Naomi enjoy shopping in?* (A second-hand shop). 2 *What is the problem with one of the items of clothing?* (They are damaged). 3 *What are the friends planning to do?* (Go shopping).

> Key: 1 C, 2 A, 3 A, 4 B, 5 B, 6 C, 7 C

Track 03
Jack: I like your jacket Naomi.
Naomi: Thank you. I bought it in a **second-hand** shop. I also got this hoodie there. It was a **bargain**. It only cost £5. I love **buying** clothes in that shop.
Jack: I need a new pair of trousers. I find **shopping** so tiring.
Naomi: I saw some nice men's trousers **for sale** in the department store when I was shopping with my dad.
Jack: Great! I'm going to get some.
Helen: What did you buy in the shops?
Adam: I got this shirt, it was **on sale** for £10. I also got these shoes and this pair of jeans.
Helen: I love **buying** new clothes! Oh wait – look at this – the jeans are **damaged**.
Adam: Oh. No!
Helen: Don't worry. **Returning** them won't be difficult as long as you have the **receipt**. The **shop assistant** will let you **exchange** them for something else or you will get the **cash** back.
Ben: What shall we do next?
Jane: I fancy **going** to the outdoor market. There's a stall with **second-hand** books I'd like **to visit**.
Ben: Good idea. I want to **buy** some trainers.
Jane: We can get them in the department store on Oxford Street.
Ben: OK, let's finish our coffee and cake and then we can go!
Alex: How was your weekend?
Rita: It was great. Yesterday I went to the craft market in Altrincham. I found a great stall with hand-made jewellery. The **prices** were very **reasonable**. There was also a stall that had **luxury** bags **for sale**.
John: I want to **go** to that market. I've never been. What did you do on Saturday?
Rita: More **shopping**, but for food in the supermarket and then in the afternoon I worked on my project and in the evening I read a book. **Reading** is one of the most relaxing things to do.
John: Yes, I like reading but I prefer **watching** TV at night.
Henry: So what do you like **doing** in your free time?
Amy: I enjoy **shopping**, especially in vintage shops, but my favourite activity is **drawing**. I love **drawing** flowers.
Henry: Really?
Amy: Yes, I draw with pen and then sometimes I paint the flowers. I like **going** to the flower market at the end of the day to buy flowers. The **prices** are usually **reduced** at that time. Then I draw the flowers. It's great fun. What about you? What's your favourite hobby?
Henry: **Swimming**. I love it.
Jessica: Can you tell me where the department store is?
Man: Yes, of course. Which one do you **want to go** to?
Jessica: John Lewis.
Man: OK. Straight down Scott Street. Turn right at the end of the road. **Walking** down Portland Street you'll see John Lewis is in between the bookshop and the bakery. It's opposite the theatre.
Jessica: All right, thank you very much.
Harry: What are you going **to do** during the school holidays?
Anna: **Studying**. I'm going to stay at home and study for the exams. What about you?
Harry: I will go to the beach and do some **shopping** in town. I asked my mum **to buy** me a new computer as mine isn't working.
Anna: Go to Computer World – there are lots of computers **on sale**. The **prices** have been **reduced** and they don't **cost** much.

3 Learners ask and answer the questions. Ask pairs to share their ideas with the class.

Skills 2: Reading and writing
Using the worksheet
- This worksheet provides reading and writing skills practice in understanding a text about Harrods.

1 Learners read the text. Ask learners what they think of the text. Have any of them been to Harrods? If not, would they like to go?

> Key: 1 H, 2 D, 3 G, 4 E, 5 B

2 Learners write about a famous department store in their country. They can use the Internet to research facts and print out pictures and stick them next to their sentences. Ask individuals to share their ideas.

25

3 Vocabulary 1

1 Look at the pictures. Then cross out the letters and use them to write the shopping words. Use the remaining letters to find the secret word.

A A A A A A
B
C C C C C C
D D
E E E E
G G
H H H
I I I I
N N N
O
P P P
R R R R
S S S S S S
T T T T

1. _____
2. _____
3. _____
4. _____
5. _____
6. _____

2 Complete the text with the correct words. The first letter is given to help you.

Last week there were lots of sales in the shops so I decided to go shopping with my friends. We went to the department store where my sister works as a **(1)** s_____ a_____. The **(2)** p_____ in the shops are really low. I found a great pair of trainers. They were a **(3)** b_____. They were reduced from £50 to £20! I also paid with my **(4)** c_____ c_____ because I didn't have any **(5)** c_____ and I got a 10% discount.

Grammar 1

1 Work in groups. Play the board game.

Instructions
- Play in groups.
- Each group needs a dice.
- Each learner needs a counter. Cut out a small piece of paper from your notebook and write your initials on it.
- One learner throws the dice and moves their counter forward by the number on the dice.
- When you land on a place use the prompts to make up a sentence. If you can't make a sentence you have to go back to START.
- If you land on a blank square make up your own sentence. Use the verbs in the box to help you.

1 I/can't imagine/move/ to Antarctica	**2** Helen doesn't mind/ help/me/with my homework	**3** The shop owner/plan/ reduce/ the prices	**4**	**5** We/enjoy/ get/bargains/ in the sales
6 I avoid/ carry/a lot of cash on me	**7** Tom/agree/ use/credit cards to pay for things is convenient	**8** You won £100. Go forward three spaces and spend it!	**9** He / suggest/go/ to the new department store	**10** She/ promise/clean/ the house
11 You haven't got cash! Go back four spaces	**12** Carol/ like/work/as a shop assistant	**13** I prefer/ watch/ documentaries to dramas	**14**	**15** I/hate/ check/receipts
16 Jessica/ plan/read/ the new Harry Potter book	**17**	**18** I /'d like/ visit/Rome	**19** He/ask/ watch/TV	**20** You spent too much money with your credit card. Go back 4!
21	**22** I/love/ read/books	**23** He'd like/be/ a footballer	**24** You have won £50. Go forward three!	**26** I/plan/ visit/my grandparents in New York
28	**29** I /can't imagine/ spend/ a lot of money on clothes	**30** Molly/ avoid/go/ to the sales because the shops are very crowded		

start agree promise suggest decide

PHOTOCOPIABLE   Power Up TRB6 © Cambridge University Press and UCLES 2018

3 Vocabulary 2

1 Match the two parts of the words. Then use the words to complete the sentences.

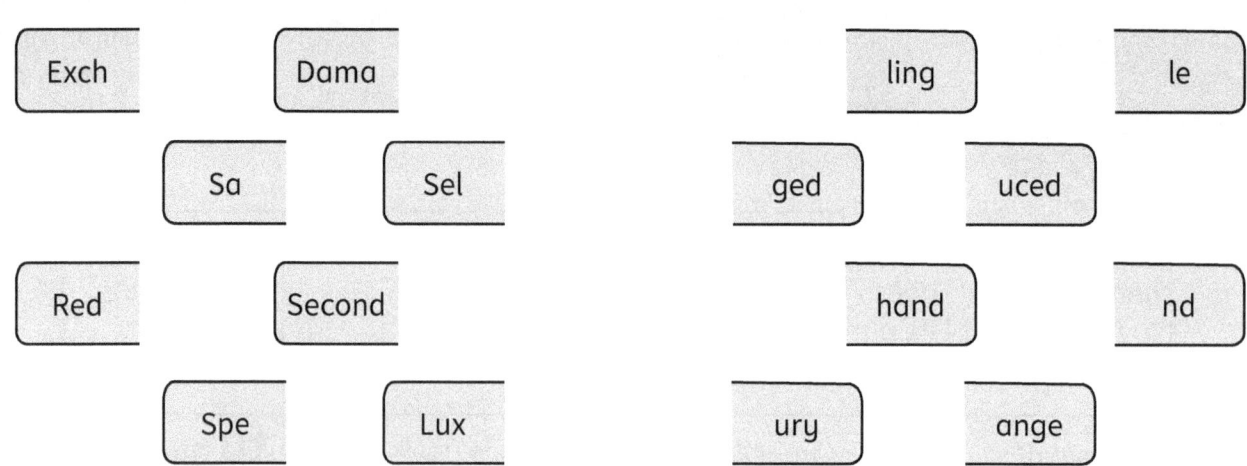

1. I bought a _____ jacket in that shop. I don't mind that it belonged to someone else.
2. The shop have _____ their prices by 50%.
3. The shoes Maria bought were _____ so she took them back to the shop.
4. My mum bought my dad a _____ watch for his 40th birthday.
5. I changed my mind about the top I bought and took it back. The shop assistant allowed me to _____ it for a different one.
6. Paul doesn't want to _____ a lot of money so he isn't going to the concert.
7. I saw a cool pair of trainers for _____ at the market.
8. That shop is _____ everything at low prices because they are closing down.

2 Complete the text with the correct words.

Blog

There was a **(1)** _ a _ _ _ at the department store and I bought a pair of shoes. They were a really **(2)** _ e _ _ _ _ _ b _ _ price so am quite pleased. They **(3)** _ _ _ t just £30. I try not to **(4)** _ p _ _ _ too much money on clothes and shoes. Usually I buy my clothes from **(5)** _ _ c _ _ _ _ _ n _ shops. I don't mind they have been used before. You can find some really amazing things in those shops. I found a shop **(6)** _ _ l l _ _ _ hats and jewellery from the 1920s! Sometimes the clothes are damaged if they are very old, but when that happens the price is usually **(7)** _ e _ _ _ e _.

3 Grammar 2

1 Look at the pictures and complete the sentences with the correct verbs.

1 _____ for new clothes can be fun.

2 _____ exercise is good for your health.

3 Peter is interested in _____ about art.

4 I enjoy _____ mountains.

5 They love _____ chess.

2 Complete the text with the correct form of the verbs from the box.

walk   sell   buy   wear   shop   look

Camden Market in London is one of the biggest markets in the city. **(1)** _____ at the market is popular attraction for tourists. There are over 1000 stalls **(2)** _____ clothes shoes, jewellery, food and lots of other items. There are stalls, which have luxury items like watches, but most things at the market have a reasonable price. People love **(3)** _____ things at the market. Many celebrities like **(4)** _____ around Camden Market. You might see Madonna, Emma Watson or even Robert Pattison **(5)** _____ at the stalls. For those of you who are keen on **(6)** _____ vintage fashion, the market has lots of stalls with second-hand and vintage items for sale.

3 Complete the sentences with the gerund form so they are true about you. Share your sentences with your partner.

1 I'm interested in _____

2 I enjoy _____

3 I'm not keen on _____

4 _____ is my favourite activity because _____

Skills 1: Listening and speaking

1 🎧 03 **Write the correct answer for each question.**

1 What is Jack going to buy? _____
2 Which item is damaged? _____
3 Where are the friends? _____
4 What did Rita do yesterday? _____
5 What's the girl's favourite hobby? _____
6 What's the boy's favourite hobby? _____
7 Where is the department store? _____
8 Where is the girl going to do during the holidays? _____

2 **Work in pairs. Ask and answer the questions.**

1 Do you enjoy shopping? Why? Why not?
2 Where do you usually buy your clothes, shoes and accessories?
3 Do you ever shop in second hand shops? What do you buy?
4 Do you prefer large department stores or small shops and markets?
5 What shops in your town would you recommend to visitors?

Skills 2: Reading and writing

1 **Choose the correct answer for each question.**
Five sentences have been removed from the article. Choose the sentences (A–H) to fill each gap (1–5). There are three extra sentences which you do not need to use.

Harrods is a **luxury** department store in London. **(1)** _____ The store was started in 1824 by Charles Harrod. At that time it was just a small room in a building **selling** curtains and material for covering furniture. Soon Charles built up and expanded the business and it became a successful shop with perfumes, clothes, medicine, clothes, shoes and groceries **for sale**. **(2)** _____ Despite this bad luck Charles managed to deliver his customers' orders in time for Christmas. He built a new shop and the store continued to grow until it became the most famous shop in the world. The author A. A. Milne who created the Winnie the Pooh books was inspired by a teddy bear he bought in the department store for his son. **(3)** _____
  Today Harrod's has 330 departments and 32 restaurants. Harrods even has its own bank, which offers **credit cards**. Many celebrities do their shopping there. You might see some of your favourite stars there.
  Shopping at Harrods is lots of fun. The shop **promises to make** it an amazing experience. Harrods is a part of British culture and the shop has many items, which are typically British like toy cars, teddy bears and lots of souvenirs. If you **decide to visit** Harrods on your next trip make sure you stop at the Toy department. **(4)** _____ London make sure you Although many of the items **cost** a lot of money there are still a few things that are **on sale** at r**easonable prices**. One of the busiest days of the year for Harrods is the first day of the sales on 26 December. People come from all over the world, often arriving in the early hours of the morning and waiting for hours in a long queue. **(5)** _____

A He started it with just two assistants.
B It is worth the wait because all the items have reduced prices and you can find some fantastic bargains
C There was a pet shop with lots of exotic animals.
D Then, in December 1883 the shop was destroyed in a fire.
E It has the biggest collection of stuffed animals in the world.
F It's a very expensive shop.
G The bear later went on to become the famous character in the books.
H It's one of the most famous department stores in the world.

2 **Think about famous department store in your country. Make notes in your notebook.**

1 What is it called?
2 When was it opened?
3 Who started the store?
4 What did it sell?
5 What does it sell today?

Mission Stage 1:
A city shopping travel guide

1 Choose a city and research its shopping rules.

City	Currency	Shopping	Payment methods

2 Write five facts about shopping in your hometown.

1 _____
2 _____
3 _____
4 _____
5 _____

4 Getting about

Vocabulary 1

Using the worksheet

- This worksheet provides practice of the core words: *gate, duty-free, exchange-rates, take off, check in, land, pilot, flight, departures, arrivals, boarding pass, check in, announcements.*

1 Learners work in pairs. They match the two parts of the words, then label the pictures. Before they start the task, ask learners what they can see in the pictures.

Key: 1 b take off, 2 d boarding pass, 3 a check in, 4 f exchange rate, 5 c duty-free

2 Learners work individually. They read the text and write the correct words on the lines. Fast finishers write the words with definitions in their notebooks.

Key: 1 pilot, 2 departures, 3 arrivals, 4 land, 5 flights, 6 announcement, 7 took off, 8 exchange-rate

Optional follow-up activity (extension):

Divide the class into pairs. Give each pair a piece of paper with a 'getting about' word written on it. Explain that they have to think of a short drama scene to describe the word. For example, if the word is 'pilot', two learners could pretend to be pilots flying a plane. They then act out their scenes for another pair to guess.

Grammar 1

Using the worksheet

- This worksheet provides practice of the target language of passives.

Key: 1 A bar of chocolate was bought in the duty-free shop. 2 My boarding pass was checked. 3 The plane was flown from Manchester to New York. 4 Information about the flight is given by the pilot. 5 10,000 people are employed by the airline. 6 Our names were called in the announcement. 7 My bag was checked at security. 8 Passengers are told their gate number in the announcement. 9 The boarding passes have been left at home. 10 I was asked to show my boarding pass in the duty-free shop. 11 Shoes are sold in this duty-free shop. 12 An announcement was made at the airport. 13 A blanket is given to every passenger. 14 A new arrivals hall has been built at the airport. 15 Our flight hasn't been cancelled. 16 She was stopped because she had keys in her pocket. 17 Sally's boarding pass has been stolen. 18 This airport is called Batman airport. 19 Lunch is served on the flight. 20 Mobile phones were switched off before the flight took off. 21 We were robbed outside the airport. 22 The passengers are given their boarding passes at the check-in desk. 23 Tenzing-Hillary Airport was built in 1964. 24 Our luggage was checked at the check-in desk. 25 The plane was landed by the pilot.

Optional follow-up activity (reinforcement):

Divide the class into two teams. Play 'Write It Up'. Brainstorm some of the vocabulary learners have learnt in Vocabulary 1 and write them on the board. Each team has to write a passive sentence with any of the words. The first team to write a correct sentence gains a point. When teams have used words on the board rub them out. Repeat with remaining words.

Vocabulary 2

Using the worksheet

- This worksheet provides practice of the core vocabulary: *passport, backpacker, tram, ferry, tour guide, ambulance, guidebook, waiting room, tunnel, luggage.*

1 Learners find and circle the words.

Key: tram, ambulance, tour guide, ferry, backpacker, passport, luggage, waiting room, tunnel, guidebook

2 Learners match the descriptions to the pictures and then write the words under the pictures.

Key: 1 D passport, 2 E backpacker, 3 F tram, 4 G ferry, 5 B tour guide, 6 I ambulance, 7 H guidebook, 8 L waiting room, 9 J tunnel, 10 A luggage

3 Learners read the text and complete the words. Fast finishers can write sentences in their notebooks.

Key: 1 tour guide, 2 guidebook, 3 ferry, 4 backpacker, 5 tunnel

Optional follow-up activity (extension):

Play an oral word association game. You need a small ball. Throw it to a learner and call out one of the core TV/film genres. The learner with the ball says a word linked to the genre and throws it to another learner. The next learner says a word linked to the previous word, and so on.

Grammar 2

Using the worksheet

- This worksheet provides practice of the target language phrasal verbs and the object.

1 Learners work in pairs. They read the gapped sentences and use the words given to complete the sentences. There is more than one possible answer for some sentences.

33

> Key: 1 to put away my passport/to put my passport away 2 to put her jumper on because it's getting cold/to put on her jumper because it's getting cold 3 gave back her favourite book 4 don't like to throw away food, 5 so keep the dog in 6 checked the luggage in/checked in the luggage

2 Learners find and correct the mistakes in the sentences. Some sentences can have more than one answer.

> Key: 1 (took off them) took them off, 2 (to food throw away) to throw away food/throw food away 3 (gave back them) gave them back 4 (the lights turn off) turn off the lights/turn the lights off 5 looking, 6 (got the tram off) got off the tram

3 Learners work in pairs. Each pair looks at the pictures and phrasal verbs, then makes up their own sentences.

> Key: **Suggested answers** 1 The teacher told us to turn off our phones./The teacher told us to turn our phones off. 2 She put on a costume for the party./She put a costume on for the party. 3 He cleaned up the mess./He cleaned the mess up. 4 The dog gave the ball back./The dog gave back the ball. 5 I tidied my sock drawer up./I tidied up my sock drawer.

Optional follow-up activity (reinforcement):
Divide the class into groups of five or six. Give each group several sheets of A4 paper. Write four or five phrasal verbs from the unit on the board. Ask each group to write a sentence with the phrasal verb. Then they write each word of the sentence on an A4 sheet in big letters. Each group takes turns to come to the front. Each member of the group holds up a word and they arrange themselves into the correct word order for that sentence.

Skills 1: Listening and speaking

Using the worksheet

- This worksheet provides listening and speaking skills practice talking about getting around. The listening skill is listening for specific information.

1 Play the audio for learners to listen. Ask a gist question for each audio to check understanding, e.g. Where is Peter? (At the airport). Play the audio a second time, pausing for learners to write their answers.

> Key: 1 Amsterdam, 2 FH 4JKL 3 11:30, 4 21 5 guidebook

Track 04
Peter: Hello, is this departures?
Assistant: Yes – how can I help you?
Peter: I'm trying to find out where I have to go to check in.
Assistant: Of course. Where are you travelling to?
Peter: Amsterdam.
Assistant: What is your flight number?
Peter: FH 4JKL
Assistant: OK. That flight will take off at 11:30. Passengers for that flight are checked in at desk 54. You'll get your boarding pass at that desk.
Peter: Great, and after that where do I go?
Assistant: After your luggage has been checked in you can go to the gate. At the moment it's Gate 21 but do listen to the announcements as sometimes the gate number is changed. But first you have to go through security. After your bags are checked you can go through to the duty-free shops.
Peter: Is there somewhere I can exchange money? I need to get some euros.
Assistant: Yes. There is bureau de change which offers good rates. You will see it when you pass the duty-free shops.
Peter: Are there any restaurants?
Assistant: Yes, there are several. There's a great Japanese restaurant I often go to. You should try it.
Peter: Are there any bookshops? I'd like to get a guidebook about Holland.
Assistant: Yes, there is one bookshop.
Peter: That's great. I'll have a look at the laptops as I need a new one. I know they are cheaper in the duty-free shops. Thank you for your help.
Assistant: Have a great flight! Oh, sir! Don't leave your passport behind!
Peter: Oh! Thank you!

2 Learners look at the pictures and describe what they can see.

3 Learners ask and answer the questions. Ask pairs to share their ideas with the class.

Optional follow-up activity (extension):
Play Noughts and Crosses. Draw a nine-square grid on the board. Number each square in the grid from 1–9. Assign each square the following questions:

1 *Where does Peter need to go first?* (The check-in desk)
2 *What number is the check-in desk?* (54) 3 *What will Peter get at the check-in desk?* (A boarding pass) 4 *Why should Peter listen to the announcements?* (Because his gate number might be changed) 5 *Where will Peter go after he has been through security?* (The duty-free shops)
6 *What currency does Peter need?* (Euros) 7 *What kind of restaurant does the assistant recommend?* (Japanese)
8 *What does Peter want to look at in the duty free shops?* (Laptops and a guidebook) 9 *What did Peter leave behind?* (His passport)

Divide the class into two teams. Assign each team as noughts or crosses. Explain that to win each team needs to get a row of either noughts or crosses in any direction.

Skills 2: Reading and writing

Using the worksheet

- This worksheet provides reading and writing skills practice in understanding a text about a gap year traveller's experiences in Mexico.

1 Learners read the text. Ask learners what they think.

> Key: 1 C, 2 A, 3 A, 4 C, 5 D

2 Learners write about a famous city or area in their country. They can use the Internet to research facts and print out pictures for each sentences.

Vocabulary 1

1 Match the two parts of the words then label the pictures.

1 take   a in
2 boarding   b off
3 check   c free
4 exchange   d pass
5 duty   f rates

a _____

b _____

c _____

d _____

e _____

2 The words in bold are used incorrectly in the text. Write the correct words on the lines.

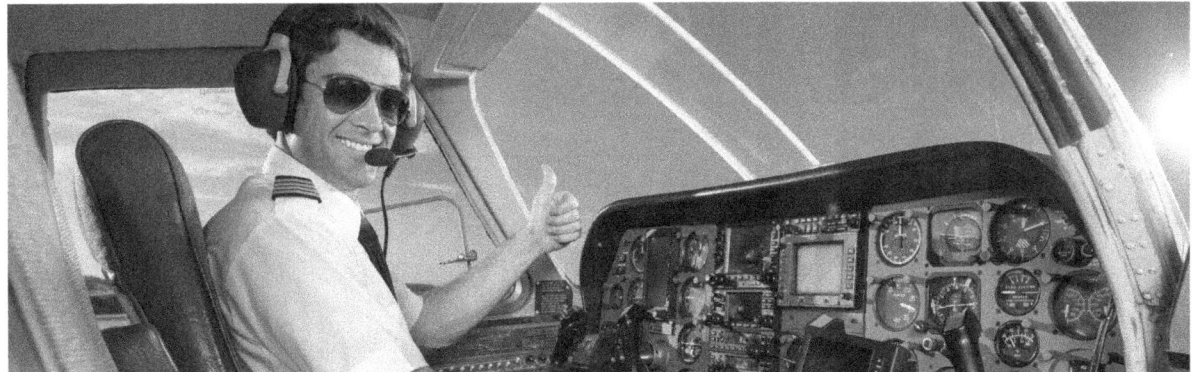

My dad is a **(1) gate** _____. He flies all over the world every week. We sometimes go with him to the **(2) arrivals** _____ part of the airport to say goodbye and come and welcome him home at **(3) departures** _____. I like watching my dad **(4) check in** _____ his plane. It looks amazing! Once I went on one of my dad's **(5) boarding passes** _____. I felt so happy and proud when he made an **(6) arrival** _____ after we **(7) landed** _____ and were high up in the air he said, 'There's a boy called Charlie sitting in seat 16 A. That's my son. It's his birthday today. Happy birthday, Charlie!' Everyone started clapping and wishing me happy birthday. When dad goes to different airports he often does shopping in the **(8) exchange rate** _____ shops. He always brings us back something special. My dad is such a great guy!

PHOTOCOPIABLE   Power Up TRB 6 © Cambridge University Press and UCLES 2018   35

4 Grammar 1

1 Play the card game.

Instructions
- Play in small groups of three.
- Cut out the cards and place them face down in a pile.
- Each learner takes turns to pick up a card and read out the active sentence and then converts it to a passive sentence.
- If they are correct they can keep the card.
- If the passive sentence is incorrect they have to put the card at the bottom of the pile.
- The winner is the learner with the most cards at the end of the game.

1 She has bought a bar of chocolate at the duty-free shop.	2 He checked my boarding pass.	3 The pilot flew the plane from Manchester to New York.	4 The pilot gives information about the flight.	5 The airline employs 10,000 people.
6 The assistant called our names in the announcement.	7 The man at security checked my bag.	8 The woman on the plane showed me to my seat.	9 I've left the boarding passes at home.	10 A cashier in the duty-free shop asked me to show her my boarding pass.
11 This duty-free shop sells shoes.	12 Jessica made an announcement at the airport.	13 The airline gives every passenger a blanket.	14 The airport has built a new arrivals hall.	15 The airline hasn't cancelled our flight.
16 The security guard stopped her because she had keys in her pocket.	17 A man has stolen Sally's boarding pass.	18 People call this airport Batman airport.	19 We serve lunch on the flight.	20 Everyone switched off their mobile phones before the flight took off.
21 A man robbed us outside the airport.	22 The assistant at the check-in desk gives the passengers their boarding passes.	23 Edmond Hillary built Tenzing-Hillary Airport on Mt Everest in 1964.	24 The woman at the check-in desk checked in our luggage.	25 The pilot landed the plane.

4 Vocabulary 2

1 Circle the words found in the word snake.

jhshytramnjsbambulancehdgsftourguidenbgshfferryqoibackpackerhsgpassportjhgskluggagemnbswhfwaitingroomnsbdhgatunnelouwjshhsguidebookhjgfdsaq

2 Match the descriptions to the pictures. Then label the pictures.

1 a small book with your photograph, nationality, date of birth and nationality
2 a person that travels to different places and carries their things in a large bag on their back
3 a transport vehicle that takes you to different places in a city
4 the word for all the bags you take on holiday
5 a person that shows you around a place
6 a place people wait for a form of transport

3 Complete the text with five words from Activity 1.

Rebecca went to Venice for the first time with her family five years ago and fell in love with it. Since then she has visited the city three times and this summer she is working there as a **(1)** _____ showing tourists around the city. Rebecca knows a lot about Venice and is thinking of writing a **(2)** _____ one day.

After landing at Marco Polo Airport she will take a kind of **(3)** _____ called a vaporetto, which takes you into the city by water. She is planning to travel around Italy as a **(4)** _____ and also go hiking in the Dolomites mountains. She likes to travel by train so that she can talk to people and see how the landscape changes. When she returns to London in September she is going to take the train from London and travel to France through the **(5)** _____.

4 Grammar 2

1 **Choose five words from each box to complete the sentences. There could be more than one answer. Write the correct answers on the lines.**

1 My father told me _____

(off   put   to   passport   away   my   puts)

2 She's going to _____

(put   it's   on   getting   cold   because   a   jumper   up   myself)

3 Yesterday he _____

(back   her   book   favourite   gave   she   flights)

4 They don't _____

(do   in   throw   to   food   like   away)

5 It will rain _____

(keep   so   dog   the   in   now   yesterday   up)

6 She has already _____

(in   checked   check   luggage   has   the   me)

2 **Find and correct the mistakes in the sentences.**

1 His clothes were wet so he took off them.
   _____

2 Sally hates to food throw away.
   _____

3 The assistant took our passports and then gave back them later.
   _____

4 Don't forget to off when you leave the room.
   _____

5 We got the tram off at the wrong stop.
   _____

3 **Work in pairs. Look at the pictures and use the words in the box to say sentences. There is more than one answer for each picture.**

(give back   clean up   turn off   put on   put away)

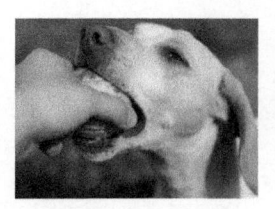

4 Skills 1: Listening and speaking

1 🎧 04 **For each question, write the correct answer in the gap. Write one or two words or a number. You will hear an assistant talking to a passenger at an airport.**

1 Peter is travelling to _____.
2 His flight number is _____.
3 The flight takes off at _____.
4 The gate number is _____.
5 Peter wants a _____ about Holland.

2 Work in pairs. Look at the pictures and describe what you can see.

> In this picture I can see …

> I can also see …

3 Work in pairs. Ask and answer the questions.

1 Have you ever travelled by airplane or ferry?
2 Where did you go?
3 Did you like it? Why? Why not?
4 How do you get around in new places?
5 Do you enjoy visiting new places? Why? Why not?

4 Skills 2: Reading and writing

1 Read the text and questions below. For each question, circle the correct letter A, B, C or D.

It's day 28 of my round-the-world trip. I remember when I **was dropped** at **departures** at London Heathrow. I felt scared and excited at the same time. Sometimes travelling can be stressful. I used to hate flying but I had overcome that. I **kept on** thinking about my family and how much I would miss them, but what scared me the most was the idea of being alone in new places. After I **checked** my **luggage in** and I **was given** my **boarding pass**. I went through **security** and into the area with the **duty-free** shops where I bought myself a **guidebook** to **look up** useful information about my first destination – Mexico. Mexico City is one of the biggest cities in the world. There are museums, markets, historic buildings, and many more attractions. I went on a walking tour of the city. Our **tour guide** really **looked after us** and **pointed out** places of interest to us. I enjoyed the walk around Chapultepec Park. There is a castle, museums, a zoo and a lake. The castle **was built** in 1785 for the Spanish Royal family. The best part of the tour was the Frida Kahlo Museum. The museum is the blue house where Mexican artist Frida Kahlo lived with her husband, the painter Diego Rivera. The paintings **are displayed** all around the house.

I met lots of other **backpackers** who were staying at the same hostel as me. It was nice to make new friends and share travel stories. After that I went to Cancun with some of my new friends. Cancun is a beautiful seaside resort. We took a **ferry** from Cancun to Isla Perez – an island, which is great for diving and snorkelling.

I visited a small town near Cancun called Puerto Morelos, where traditional clothes are worn by the local women. The clothes were bright and colourful. Many beautiful crafts **are made** in this town. I also went to Tulum, which has some of the most famous Mayan sites in the world. Tulum was an important city until 1518 when it **was destroyed**. Today it's one of the most beautiful and relaxing places in Mexico with its beautiful beaches.

So far I have had an amazing time in Mexico. Today I am **leaving** Mexico **behind**. The next part of my trip is Belize. At the moment I'm waiting at my **gate** for my **flight**!

1 Jessica was most scared about …
   A flying
   B missing her family
   C facing a new adventure on her own
   D travelling

2 Which was Jessica's favourite place in Mexico City?
   A the Frida Kahlo Museum
   B the walking tour
   C Chapultepec Park
   D the markets

3 What does Jessica say about Isla Perez?
   A the water was great for diving
   B she made friends there
   C the women wore traditional clothes
   D she bought hand-made crafts there

4 What does Jessica think of Tulum?
   A It's very hot
   B It's an important Mayan city
   C It's beautiful and relaxing
   D the Mayan ruins are very famous

5 A good title to this article would be …
   A My guide to the Mayan ruins of Mexico
   B A guide to the world
   C A museum tour of Mexico City
   D A month spent discovering Mexico

4 Mission Stage 1: A travel guide

1 Choose a country and plan how to get there. Write a travel checklist.

Travel Checklist

Group name:

Country:

Trip:

Transport:

Cost:

Times:

2 If you could go on any trip in the world, what would it be? Why?

_____
_____
_____
_____

5 Study smarter

Vocabulary 1

Using the worksheet

- This worksheet provides practice of the core words: *certificate, course, essay, mark, level, information, instructions, project, test, term*.

  Learners work individually to find and circle the words in the word snake. They then use the extra letters to write the secret word and complete the sentences.

> Key: certificate, course, mark, test, level, project, essay, information, term
>
> Secret word instructions:
> 1 project, 2 essay, 3 test, 4 mark,
> 5 certificate, 6 information, 7 course, 8 term,
> 9 level, 10 instructions

Optional follow-up activity (extension):
Learners write incomplete sentences using the environment vocabulary. They copy their gapped sentences out neatly and swap them with a partner to write the missing words.

Grammar 1

Using the worksheet

- This worksheet provides practice of the target language of past simple and present perfect with time phrases.
1 Learners work in pairs and look at the pictures and write sentences using the past simple or present simple. Before the start you could elicit what learners can see in the pictures.

> Key: 1 I have been to Paris many times. 2 Did you walk the dog this morning? 3 Alex hasn't finished his essay yet. 4 Did you do a Spanish course last term? 5 Jack has just passed his swimming test.

2 Learners read the sentences and correct the mistakes in the sentences.

> Key: 1 (have been) was 2 (not decided) hasn't decided 3 (never tried) have never tried 4 (just have finished) have just finished 5 (not read) hasn't read

3 Learners play the game in pairs. They ask each other questions using *Have you ever …?* And the ideas in the box. Explain that they have to answer *Yes* to each question and their partner has to ask questions using the past simple to find out if their partner is lying.

Optional follow-up activity (reinforcement):
Write the following time phrases on the board: *since, yet, just, last weekend, last week, never, last year, for two weeks*. Divide the class into two teams. Assign a team a time phrase and ask them to write a sentence using the time phrase and the correct tense. The first team to finish gains a point. Each team can then check the other team's sentence. Repeat with the other time phrases.

Vocabulary 2

Using the worksheet

- This worksheet provides practice of the core vocabulary: *excited, disappointed, confused, nervous, worried, delighted, interested, confident, calm, bored*.
1 Learners read the sentences, underline the adjectives and draw a ☺ or ☹ face to show if the adjective is positive or negative.

> Key: 1 I am excited about the art course that I'm starting next term. ☺ 2 Julie was disappointed with the mark she got on her essay. ☹ 3 Peter was confused by the instructions for the computer. ☹ 4 Alice has felt nervous since she found out about the test. ☹ 5 John is worried about the project. ☹ 6 My teacher is delighted about my mark. ☺ 7 Since I went to Italy I have been interested in learning Italian. ☺ 8 I feel confident about the exam. ☺ 9 Doing yoga makes me feel calm. ☺ 10 The film made me feel bored. ☹

2 Learners read the clues and write the words.

> Key: 1 excited, 2 delighted, 3 interested, 4 disappointed, 5 worried, 6 confident

3 Learners complete the sentences about them and then share the sentences with their partner. Ask a few pairs to share their sentences with the class.

Optional follow-up activity (extension):
Play 'Mime It'. Divide the class into two teams. Invite a member from each team to the front and whisper an adjective to them. They go back to their team and mime the word for their team to guess.

Grammar 2

Using the worksheet

- This worksheet provides practice of the target language of the past perfect.

1 Learners look at the pictures and write sentences with the past simple and past perfect. Before they start you could ask learners what they can see in the pictures. You could elicit the answer for the first picture and write it on the board.

> Key: 1 Hannah was delighted because she had won the race. 2 Frank was worried because he had lost his phone. 3 Harry had a stomach ache because she had eaten too much ice cream. 4 Liz was disappointed because she had got a bad mark in the essay. 5 Chloe was excited because her parents had bought her a bike.

2 Learners complete the text with the correct form of the verbs in the box.

> Key: 1 travelled, 2 hadn't flown, 3 told, 4 spent, 5 had read, 6 hadn't finished building, 7 lived, 8 hadn't booked

3 Learners work in small groups of three and cut out the cards. They take turns to read out the situations and give an explanation using the past perfect. Each learner should give a different explanation.

Optional follow-up activity (reinforcement):

Learners write eight sentences about activities they did last weekend using the past simple. Explain that they should write the sentences in jumbled order of the events. Then their partner has to guess the order of the activities by saying the sentences using the past perfect, e.g. *I had my breakfast. I had a shower. I played football. I did my homework. I met my friends. I went to the cinema. I cleaned my bedroom. I did my homework.* Their partner can then say *You had had your shower before you ate your breakfast. You had done your homework before you played football.*

Skills 1: Listening and speaking

Using the worksheet

- This worksheet provides listening and speaking skills to practise talking about education. The listening skill is listening for specific information.

1 Play the audio for learners to listen. Ask a gist question about the audio to check understanding, e.g. *Where are Karen and James?* (In the library)

> Key: 1 B, 2 B, 3 C, 4 B, 5 B

Track 05

Karen: What are you doing?
James: **I've just finished** my **essay**.
Karen: What is it about?
James: Bumble bees.
Karen: **I did a project** about bumble bees last **term**.
James: Have you studied for the science **test**?
Karen: No, **I haven't started yet**. I am a bit confused by the chapter on the environment. I feel confident about animals and insects because **I have read** a lot about them.
James: I'm a bit **worried** because I **got** a bad **mark** on the last test. It's because **I had been** ill for a week before and **hadn't slept** very well the night before the test. But I also **hadn't studied** enough. Have you got any other study tips? **I have tried** making notes, memorising facts, but it doesn't work.
Karen: I do drawings with short notes.
James: I'll try that. **Have you heard** about the school trip to Scotland?
Karen: No.
James: It's been cancelled because they **hadn't booked** enough rooms. Mr Roberts tried booking in the Lake District but there wasn't a big enough hotel, so we are going to Wales.
Karen: I'm looking forward to it.

Optional follow-up activity (extension):

Draw a table on the board with two columns. Write *Karen* in the first column and *James* in the second. Play the audio again and ask specific questions about Karen and James. Learners place a tick in the correct column for each question, e.g. *Who did a project about bumble bees?* (Karen) *Who has a test?* (Karen and James) *Who is confused about something?* (Karen) *Who feels nervous about the test?* (James) *Who is going on the school trip?* (Karen and James)

Skills 2: Reading and writing

Using the worksheet

- This worksheet provides reading and writing skills practice in understanding a text about unusual schools around the world.

1 Learners read the text. Ask learners what they think of the text. Would they like to attend any of the schools?

> Key: 1 A, 2 C, 3 A, 4 B, 5 B, 6 B 7 B

2 Learners write about an unusual school in their country. They can use the Internet to research facts and print out pictures to stick next to their sentences. Ask individuals to share their ideas with the class.

Optional follow-up activity (extension):

Learners work in small groups of three, researching an unusual school. When they finish, they can create a poster and present it to the class.

5 Vocabulary 1

Find and circle the words in the shape. Then use the words to complete the sentences. What word do the extra letters spell? _____

[Word search spiral containing: COURSE, MARK, TEST, CERTIFICATE, INFORMATION, ESSAY, TERM, PROJECT, LEVEL, INSTRUCTIONS]

1 We are working on our art _____; it's about Picasso.
2 I have to write a 1000 word _____ about education.
3 The students had an English _____ on Wednesday.
4 Karl was happy because he got a good _____ in the exam.
5 Alice got a _____ after she passed the diving course.
6 I'm looking for _____ about space travel.
7 She is doing an English _____ at the college; it will last 10 weeks.
8 In the autumn _____ we are going to learn about the continents.
9 As I passed the exam I am going to move on to the next _____ in Spanish.
10 The teacher told the students to read the _____ carefully.

5 Grammar 1

1 **Look at the pictures and use the prompts to write sentences. Use the past simple or present perfect tenses.**

1 I /be/to …/many times
   _____

2 you/walk/ …/this morning?
   _____

3 Alex/not finish/his/ …/yet
   _____

4 you/do/a … course/last term?
   _____

5 Jack/pass/just/his/ …/test
   _____

2 **Work in pairs. Play the *Are you lying?* game.**

Instructions
- Learners take turns to ask each other questions using '*Have you ever …*' and the prompts in the box.
- Learners must answer '*Yes*' to the *Have you ever …* questions.
- Learners then ask three questions using the past simple to find out if their partner is lying.
- Their partner replies with the truth.

climb a mountain   fail a test   win a prize
cry at the cinema   sleep in a tent   forget a friend's birthday
meet a famous person   do a language course   travel to Paris
stay awake all night

Have you ever climbed a mountain? — Yes, I have.

What mountain did you climb? — Mount Etna.

How long did it take? — 30 minutes

I think you are lying! — Yes, I am!

PHOTOCOPIABLE   Power Up TRB 6 © Cambridge University Press and UCLES 2018   45

5 Vocabulary 2

1 Find and underline the adjectives in the sentences. Draw a ☺ face if they are positive and a ☹ face if they are negative.

1 I am excited about the art course that I'm starting next term.
2 Julie was disappointed with the mark she got on her essay.
3 Peter was confused by the instructions for the computer.
4 Alice has felt nervous since she found out about the test.
5 John is worried about the project.
6 My teacher is delighted about my mark.
7 Since I went to Italy I have been interested in learning Italian.
8 I feel confident about the exam.
9 Doing yoga makes me feel calm.
10 The film made me feel bored.

2 Read the clues in bold and write the words to complete the text. The first letter of each word is given to you.

Kelly started a dance course last term. She is learning street dance. She hopes to compete in a national dance competition next month. She's very **(1) happy and looking forward to something** e_____ about the competition. Last week she was **(2) very pleased about something** d_____ because she did very well in a performance. She's now moved on to the next level of street dance. Kelly was always **(3) wanting to know more about something** i_____ in dance. She loves dance as a way of showing her feelings. When she is **(4) to feel sad because something wasn't as good as you hoped** d_____ about something or **(5) a bit scared about something** w_____. She likes to dance. It helps her feel better. Kelly is **(6) feel sure you can do something** c_____ about the competition because she has been working hard. Before the completion she will go to bed early.

3 Read and complete the sentences about you. Then share your sentences with your partner.

1 I felt nervous when _____
2 I felt excited about _____
3 I'm interested in _____
4 I felt disappointed when _____

5 Grammar 2

1 Write sentences using the words given, plus the past simple and the past perfect.

1 (Hannah/delighted/won the race)
   _____

2 Frank/worried/lost/his phone)
   _____

3 (Harry/stomach ache/eat too much ice cream)
   _____

4 (Liz/disappointed/got a bad mark in the essay)
   _____

5 (Chloe/parents/excited/buy her a bike)
   _____

2 Complete the missing parts of the verbs. Then use the past simple or past perfect form of the verbs to complete the text.

bo ___ ___   fl ___   bui ___ ___   li ___ ___   re ___ ___   tra ___ ___ ___   spe ___ ___   te ___ ___

Last month I went to Barcelona as part of an art course I am doing. I was **delighted** when my teacher told me about the trip. We **(1)** _____ by aeroplane which was scary for me because I **(2)** _____ before. Before I left I **(3)** _____ my teacher that I was worried about the flight and she sat beside me so I wouldn't feel **nervous**. We **(4)** _____ the first day visiting the Sagrada Familia. I was very **excited** to be there because I **(5)** _____ a lot of books about the church. It is a church which was built by the architect Gaudi. The cathedral has taken over 150 years to build – Gaudi still **(6)** _____ it when he died in 1926. We also went to the Piccasso Museum. Many of the paintings are from the time when Picasso **(7)** _____ in Barcelona. There are also some of his sculptures in the museum. On the last day we went to the Museum of Contemporary Art. We studied the paintings and made our own drawings of them. The last museum we were supposed to go to was the Chocolate Museum but we couldn't go as we **(8)** _____ our tickets in advance and there wasn't enough time to join the long queue at the entrance. We were all very **disappointed** about this!

3 Read the instructions. Play the game in groups of three.

Instructions
- Place the cards face down.
- Take turns to pick up a card and read out the situation. Each learner must then give an explanation for the situation using the past perfect. Each learner has to give a different explanation.

| I got a bad mark in the test. | I feel tired this morning. | I couldn't answer the essay question. |
| I felt disappointed yesterday. | I was late for school this morning. | I couldn't get into my house last night. |

PHOTOCOPIABLE   Power Up TRB 6 © Cambridge University Press and UCLES 2018   47

5 Skills 1: Listening and speaking

1 🎧 05 **Read the questions and circle the correct answer. James and Karen are talking about studying.**

1 What is James doing?
  A he's working on a project
  B he's writing an essay
  C he's looking up information

2 Which part of the test is Karen worried about?
  A the part on insects
  B the part on the environment
  C the part on animals

3 Why is James nervous about the exam?
  A he hasn't studied
  B he is ill
  C he did badly on the last one

4 How does Karen usually study?
  A by making notes
  B by doing drawings and short notes
  C by memorising facts

5 Where are they going on a school trip to?
  A Scotland
  B Wales
  C The Lake District

2 Work in pairs. Look at the pictures and say what you can see.

In this picture I can see…

I can also see

3 Work in pairs. Ask and answer the questions.

1 What subjects at school are you interested in?
2 How do you usually study for tests?
3 Describe a time when you felt nervous at school.
4 Describe a time you felt excited at school.
5 Describe a time when you felt delighted at school.

48 Power Up TRB 6 © Cambridge University Press and UCLES 2018 **PHOTOCOPIABLE**

5 Skills 2: Reading and writing

1 For these questions circle the correct answer.

Which country:	India	Bali	England
1 has children of all ages in the same classroom?	A	B	C
2 teaches yoga?	A	B	C
3 is for children without homes?	A	B	C
4 has classrooms without walls?	A	B	C
5 teaches students to respect nature?	A	B	C
6 allows students to choose what they want to study?	A	B	C
7 has students work on projects as part of their learning?	A	B	C

Unusual schools around the world

Train Platform Schools

The first train platform school was set up by Mrs Inderjit Khurana. She **had noticed** there were lots of children at the train station. These children **were** homeless and didn't go to school, so Inderjit brought the school to them. She included **courses** on reading, writing, song and dance to make sure her students were **interested** in and **excited** about the lessons. There is just one classroom for the 100 students at the school. Over the years, more train platform schools **have opened** across India.

The Green School

Students at The Green School in Bali are taught in classrooms without walls. The school has a curriculum which focuses on nature and respect for the environment. The Green School was founded by John and Cynthia Hardy in 2006. The couple **had lived** in Bali for many years before they opened The Green School. They **had taught** their own children at home for many years. The school now has over 400 students. Students are encouraged to take part in projects which develop their creativity and problem solving skills.

Hebden Bridge School

A group of teachers in England **have just opened** a new school. Students at Hebden Bridge School practise yoga and meditation as part of their studies. Students are allowed to choose what they want to learn. They take **tests**, write **essays** and receive **certificates** for completing their courses. Students at the school are **delighted** and feel that doing yoga and meditation every day makes them feel **calm**.

2 Think about an unusual school in your country. Answer the questions.

1 What is it called? _____
2 When was it opened? _____
3 Who started the school? _____
4 What is unusual about it? _____
5 How many students are there? _____
6 Would you like to go to the school? Why? Why not? _____

5 Mission Stage 2: A class quiz

Write questions for a class quiz.

Group name: _____	Group name: _____	Group name: _____	Group name: _____
Topic: _____	Topic: _____	Topic: _____	Topic: _____
Question 1	**Question 2**	**Question 3**	**Question 4**
A	A	A	A
B	B	B	B
C	C	C	C

Group name: _____	Group name: _____	Group name: _____	Group name: _____
Topic: _____	Topic: _____	Topic: _____	Topic: _____
Question 5	**Question 6**	**Question 7**	**Question 8**
A	A	A	A
B	B	B	B
C	C	C	C

Group name: _____	Group name: _____
Topic: _____	Topic: _____
Question 9	**Question 10**
A	A
B	B
C	C

6 Good job!

Vocabulary 1

Using the worksheet

- This worksheet provides practice of the core words: *architect, cleaner, postman, programmer, publisher, musician, scientist, politician, sailor, librarian, hairdresser*.

1 Learners work individually. They find and circle the words in the word square. Then they label the pictures.

> Key: 1 scientist, 2 hairdresser, 3 programmer, 4 musician, 5 cleaner, 6 librarian, 7 publisher, 8 postman, 9 architect, 10 sailor, 11 politician

2 Learners can work in pairs. They complete the text with the correct words. Fast finishers write the words and draw a clue next to them to help them remember.

> Key: 1 hairdresser, 2 postman, 3 librarian, 4 sailors, 5 programmer

Optional follow-up activity (extension):

Play 'Relay Race'. Divide learners into teams of five and ask them to stand in lines. Give each player at the front a word card from the vocabulary set. The first player has to make up a sentence with the word and then pass it to the person behind them. This player has to make up a different sentence with the word. When the card reaches the last person in the line they run to the front, say their sentence and place the card on the table. They can then take their place at the front of the line. The first team to finish the wins.

Grammar 1

Using the worksheet

- This worksheet provides practice of the target language of modals for deduction: *must, can't, might, may, could*.

1 Learners read the sentences and cross out the incorrect options.

> Key: 1 could be/might be, 2 can't be/mustn't be 3 mustn't be/can't be, 4 must rain/can't rain 5 can't be/might be

2 Learners work in pairs. Point at the pictures and elicit what learners can see. Then learners complete the sentences using modal verbs and the words in the box.

> Key: 1 must/could/might/may be a hairdresser. 2 can't be German. 3 could/might/may be a politician. 4 can't be the countryside. 5 can't be fast.

3 Learners play the game in pairs. They secretly choose a job and then give a clue. Their partner has to guess what they are using modal verbs.

Optional follow-up activity (reinforcement):

Divide the class into groups of three. Each group member thinks of a celebrity and gives a clue about who it is without saying who it is. The other members have to guess who it is using modal verbs.

Vocabulary 2

Using the worksheet

- This worksheet provides practice of the core vocabulary: *full-time, part-time, unemployed, earn, boss, salary, colleague, staff, quit, retire, career*.

1 Learners unscramble the words in the sentences. Fast finishers can write sentences in their notebooks.

> Key: 1 full-time, 2 staff, 3 part-time, 4 retire, 5 earn, 6 colleague

2 Learners read the text and decide which words in bold are used incorrectly. They write the correct words.

> Key: 1 incorrect quit 2 correct 3 incorrect salary 4 correct 5 correct

3 Learners work in pairs. They take turns to give clues about the words for their partner to guess.

Optional follow-up activity (extension):

Divide the class into two teams. Play 'First Letters'. Ask each team to line up at the back of the room. Write the first letter of one of the vocabulary words on the board. A member from each team has to race to the board and write the word. The first to write the correct word gains a point.

Grammar 2

Using the worksheet

This worksheet provides practice of the target language of the present perfect continuous. Divide learners into groups of three. Each group needs one worksheet. Ask learners to make counters out of paper. Provide a dice for each group. Go through the instructions for the game. Demonstrate with the second square. Write a present perfect continuous sentence, i.e. *She has been studying French since 2011*. If a learner lands on a square a previous player has landed on they have to make up their own sentence using the present perfect continuous. If they land on a blank they make up a present perfect continuous sentence. They can use the verbs in the box. Learners play the game until the last player has reached the finish line.

> Key: 1 He has been working as an architect for 20 years. 2 She has been studying French since 2011. 3 Have you been watching TV all night? 4 They haven't been cleaning their bedrooms. 5 Blank square 6 Congratulations! You've got a job as a scientist. Go forward two spaces. 7 I have been working part-time as a librarian. 8 Have they been playing football this afternoon? 9 We have been publishing magazines about musicians for the last seven years. 10 Blank square 11 You quit your job. Go back three and find a new job! 12 Since I quit my job as a postman I haven't been riding my bike. 13 He has been doing the gardening since last summer. 14 Have you been studying science in the library this week? 15 Your boss has increased your salary. Go forward two 16 Blank square 17 She hasn't been doing much exercise. 18 Blank square 9. 19 She hasn't been living here for long. 20 Your colleague needs help with a project. Go back three. 21 How long has he been earning a good salary? 22 The politician has been talking for 40 minutes on TV. 23 I have been playing tennis with my boss. 24 She hasn't been travelling around Europe. 25 Congratulations! You've got a part-time job. Go forward two 26 Blank square 27 My colleague has been studying hairdressing. 28 My dad has been working as a publisher for 20 years. 29 Blank square 30 We have been making your birthday cake all afternoon.

Optional follow-up activity (reinforcement):
Learners write three present perfect continuous sentences. They include positive and negative sentences. Two are true and one should be a lie. Then they share their sentences with their partner who has to ask questions to find out which is a lie. They can ask three questions for each sentence. You can demonstrate the activity by writing three sentences about yourself, e.g. *I have been working here for 10 years, I have been living in London for two years, I haven't been eating chocolate every day.* Then learners ask you questions to find out which sentence is a lie.

Skills 1: Listening and speaking

Using the worksheet

- This worksheet provides listening and speaking skills practice talking about jobs. The listening skill is listening for specific information.

1 Play the audio for learners to listen. Ask gist questions to check understanding, e.g. 1 *What are the friends talking about?* (Their career choices for their presentations) 2 *What is Mark looking for?* (A job) 3 *How does Jenny feel about her day?* (Good)

Track 06

Chris: What job are you doing your presentation on, Mandy?
Mandy: I am not sure. I've been looking for something for two hours!
Chris: What career are you interested in?
Mandy: I like computers – maybe I could be a programmer, but I also love books, so I might become a librarian. What job do you want to do?
Chris: A musician.
Carol: Is Mark still unemployed?
Billy: Yes, he's been looking for a job for three months. He asked about a job in the post office but there aren't any. He applied for a cleaner job but he didn't get it. There was an advert looking for sailors in the newspaper and he speaks two languages so he might have a good chance with that.
Dad: How was school today?
Jenny: Great. We had a yoga class in the morning. Then we had maths. The afternoon was the most fun – we worked on our computer projects. We have been designing an app.
Dad: You are really good at programming. I think you could be a programmer in the future.
Adam: How was your weekend?
Megan: It was great. We went to Copenhagen. It's a really pretty city. On Saturday we went cycling around the city. Then on Sunday we visited some museums. In the afternoon I went to the hairdresser's because in the evening we went to the opera.
Adam: Cool! Denmark was voted the happiest country in the world. It must be a great place to live.
Sophie: The sports camp has got part-time vacancies. You can earn some extra money.
Joe: Cool. This must be where Charlotte works. She coaches tennis.
Sophie: You are great at swimming – why don't you apply to be a swimming coach.
Joe: I think I'd prefer to be a football coach. I haven't been doing swimming coaching for very long. I have more experience of coaching football.
Molly: What job does your mum do, David?
David: She's a publisher.
Molly: She must have a big salary. What about your dad?
David: He's a scientist. What do your parents do?
Molly: My mum quit her job. She's been writing a novel at home. My dad is an architect.
Helen: Have they been playing for long?
Ben: No, they just started.
Helen: Look! Isn't that Jeremy? Playing the guitar.
Ben: That can't be Jeremy. He's in Paris at the moment.
Helen: Really? It looks just like him.
Ben: It might be his brother. He's also a musician. Who's that on the drums?
Helen: It's Adam, and Kelly is singing.

Optional follow-up activity (extension):
Write some of the key vocabulary on the board from the audio, e.g. *musician, architect, career, part-time, programmer, earn.* Play the audio. Ask learners to put up their hand when they hear one of the words.

Skills 2: Reading and writing

Using the worksheet

- This worksheet provides reading and writing skills practice in understanding a text about jobs.

Learners read the text. What do learners think of it?

> Key: 1 C, 2 C, 3 A, 4 C, 5 A

6 Vocabulary 1

1 Find and circle the jobs in the puzzle. Then label the pictures with the words you find.

h	s	o	t	r	l	r	o	e	r	e
j	a	r	c	h	i	t	e	c	t	p
i	i	i	o	t	b	t	e	l	o	u
o	l	a	r	h	r	z	t	e	t	b
t	o	t	z	d	a	e	z	a	a	l
e	r	z	n	e	r	h	a	n	n	i
w	t	h	e	n	i	e	h	e	n	s
p	o	s	t	m	a	n	s	r	h	h
a	s	c	i	e	n	t	i	s	t	e
a	p	r	o	g	r	a	m	m	e	r
s	e	r	y	y	y	q	a	z	z	r

1. _____ 2. _____ 3. _____ 4. _____ 5. _____ 6. _____

7. _____ 8. _____ 9. _____ 10. _____ 11. _____

2 Complete the text with five jobs from Activity 1.

Salon requires a **1** _____ experienced in cutting and styling. We need people who are creative and excited about their work and know today's trends and celebrities' styles.

The St James secondary school is looking for a **3** _____ for the summer. You will love books and be organised, have a good memory and can look up information for people. We want people who are friendly, helpful and patient.

- Are you looking for a new challenge?
- Do you know the neighbourhoods well?
- Can you drive?

We are looking for a new **2** _____ to join our friendly team in Croydon near London.

Small IT company that makes apps designed to help you keep fit and healthy is looking for a talented, hard-working **4** _____ who knows the following computer languages: JAVA, IOS and SQL.

6 Grammar 1

1 **Cross out the incorrect options.**
1. That **can't be/could be/might be** Alice. She's in America at the moment.
2. She **can't be/mustn't be/may be** a programmer. She has made this app and knows computer languages.
3. He **could be/mustn't be/can't be** a scientist. I see him at the hospital every day.
4. It **must rain/might rain/can't rain** tomorrow. But I'm not sure.
5. She **must be/can't be/might be French**. She has a French passport.

2 **Look at the pictures and complete the sentences with the correct modal verbs and the words in the box. There is more than one answer for some sentences.**

> hairdresser   politician   countryside   fast   German

She's cutting the woman's hair, so she _____

Helen has an American passport so she _____

She's making a speech. I think she _____

There are a lot of buildings, so it _____

It's a turtle, so it _____

3 **Work in pairs. Choose one of the jobs in the box. Give a clue to your partner. Your partner has to make a true sentence with a modal of possibility.**

> musician   cleaner   librarian   programmer   postman   politician

I'm very famous.   You could be a musician.   Correct!

54

6 Vocabulary 2

1 **Unscramble the bold letters in the sentences. Write the unscrambled word.**

1. I can't work **lflu-meti** _____ because I need to look after my grandma.
2. We must have lunch at that restaurant again, the **tasff** _____ were so friendly!
3. Since Rebecca has been working **tarp-emit** _____ she is happier.
4. His dad is going to **teierr** _____ next year.
5. Politicians **raen** _____ a very good salary.
6. At work I have some great **gcolelaeus** _____.

2 **If the words in bold in the text are used correctly tick ✓ them and if they are used incorrectly cross ✗. Write the correct word on the line.**

This month we are doing a profile on Jessica, a young woman who has a big dream. She has **(1) salary** _____ her job as a programmer. Although she has a good **(2) career** _____ and earns a big **(3) colleague** _____, she wasn't happy. She wants to be a musician. Her **(4) boss** _____ encouraged Jessica to follow her dream. Jessica is **(5) unemployed** _____ at the moment but she's busy writing songs and looking for members for her band. Check back next week to find out how Jessica is getting on.

3 **Play a game with your partner. Describe a word from the box for your partner to guess.**

> colleague   staff   boss   salary   career   quit

6 Grammar 2

Play the board game in groups of three.

Instructions

- Each group needs a dice.
- Each learner needs a counter.
- One learner throws the dice and moves their counter forward by the number on the dice.
- When you land on a place, use the prompts to make up a present perfect continuous sentence. Add *since* or *for* where necessary. If you can't make a sentence, you have to go back to START.
- If you land on a blank square, make up your own present perfect continuous sentence. Use the verbs in the box to help you.

START

1. He/work/as/architect/20 years.
2. She/study/French/2011
3. She/study/French/2011
4. They/not have/clean/their bedrooms
5. Blank square
6. Congratulations! You've got a job as a scientist. Go forward two spaces.
7. I/work/part-time/as a/librarian
8. Have/they/play/football/this afternoon?
9. We/publish/magazines/about/musicians/the last seven years.
10. Blank square
11. You quit your job. Go back three and find a new job!
12. Since/I/quit/my job/a postman/not ride/my bike.
13. He/do/gardening/he/be/unemployed.
14. He/do/gardening/he/be/unemployed.
15. Your boss has increased your salary. Go forward 2
16. Blank square
17. She/not do/much/exercise
18.
19. She /have / not/live/here/long
20. Your colleague needs help with a project. Go back three.
21. How long/ have/he/earn/a good salary/?
22. The politician/talking /40 minutes/TV.
23. I/ play/ tennis/a with my boss
24. She/not travel/around/Europe
25. Congratulations! You've got a part-time job. Go forward 2
26. Blank square
27. My colleague/ study/ hairdressing
28. My dad/work/ a publisher/ 20 years
29. Blank square
30. We/making/your/birthday cake/all afternoon

You've landed on number 3

FINISH

56   Power Up TRB 6 © Cambridge University Press and UCLES 2018   **PHOTOCOPIABLE**

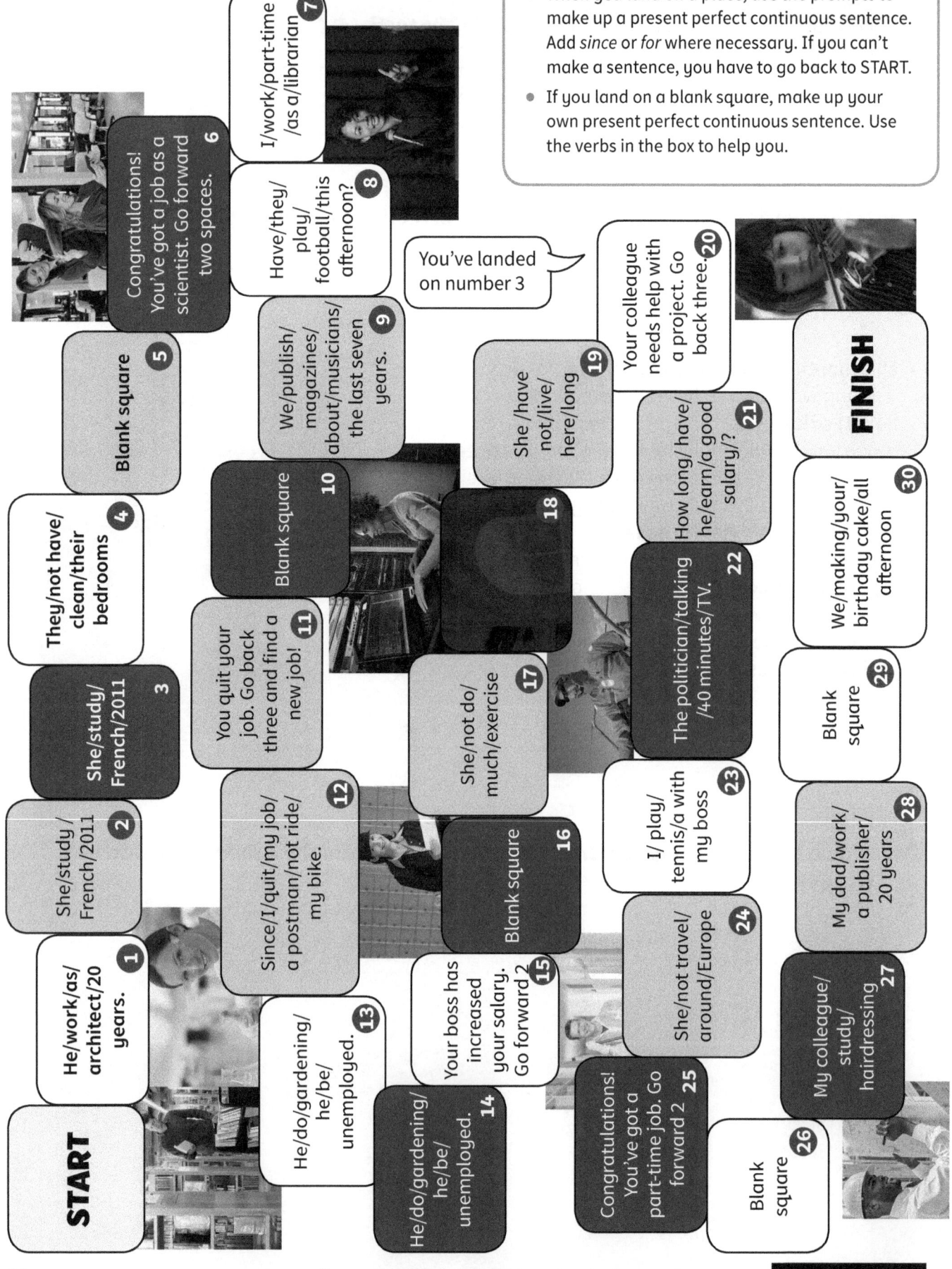

6 Skills 1: Listening and speaking

1 🎧 **Write the correct answer.**
06

1 What does Chris want to be? _____
2 What did Mandy enjoy the most? _____
3 What job does Billy think Mark will get? _____
4 What did Megan do on Sunday afternoon? _____
5 What sport does Joe want to teach? _____
6 What job does David's mum do? _____
7 Who could be Jeremy's brother? _____

2 **Work in pairs. Look at the pictures and say what you can see.**

In this picture I can see … I can also see …

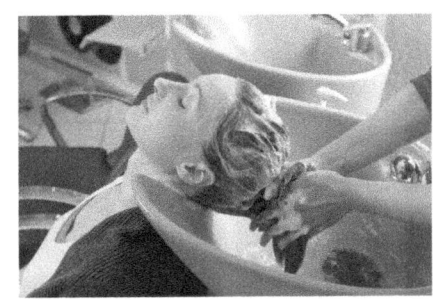

3 **Ask and answer the questions with your partner.**

1 What do you think of the jobs in the pictures?
2 Which of these jobs do you like? Why?
3 What qualities do you think you need to do each job?
4 What would be your ideal job?
5 What qualities do you have that would make you good at it?

6 Skills 2: Reading and writing

Read the text. Then read the questions and circle the correct answer.

Lego **architect** Harry Marsh talks about his job

I always loved Lego bricks. I remember when my parents bought me my first Lego set. I was so excited and immediately started building a house. As I got older the buildings and objects I built became more interesting and bigger. I love the concentration that is needed to make something. But the best thing about it is that when I'm building something I forget about all my worries. I'm so focused on my design and creating something amazing that I lose myself completely.

My dad was a **publisher** and my mum was a **programmer**. I thought I **might become** a **publisher** too as I liked reading. Then when I was a 17 I joined a band. I was the drummer. We were quite good and wanted to become famous. But then the band split up and it was time to go to university. I was good at maths and art and I loved building structures, so I did architecture.

After I finished university I worked for a few years as an architect. Then the company I was working for closed down. I was **unemployed** for some months before a friend told me about the job at Lego. I thought, that **can't be** a real job – it sounded like too much fun! The **salary** was good and the idea of making Lego models for a living really appealed to me, although I hadn't played with Lego since I was a child. There was a two-hour interview followed by a three-hour test. I did quite well at the interview but it was the test that made me lose my confidence. I had to build a boat. I was really nervous. I was certain that I had failed, but I passed!

I've been working as a Lego architect for 40 years now. It's a fun **career** and very creative. It's also hard work and sometimes very stressful. I have to travel to Legolands(R) all over the world to build different things. That can be quite tiring and has kept me away from my family over the years. But in the end I still think it's the best job in the world! I'll miss it when I retire next year.

1 Harry enjoys making Lego buildings because
   A he loves building houses
   B it makes him pay attention to what he is doing
   C he forgets about his problems
   D he can create amazing things

2 What did Harry want to be when he was 17?
   A a publisher
   B a architect
   C a musician
   D a programmer

3 Why didn't Harry feel confident about getting the job?
   A the test was difficult
   B he didn't do well at the interview
   C he hadn't played with Lego for a long time
   D because he was unemployed

4 How does Harry feel about his job now?
   A it makes him feel sad
   B he thinks it is stressful
   C he loves it
   D it is very tiring

5 What would be a good introduction to this article?
   A In this article Harry Marsh talks about his career
   B Harry Marsh tells us why he became a Lego architect
   C Harry Marsh talks about the advantages and disadvantages of his career choices
   D in this article Harry Marsh describes why he loves his job

6 Mission Stage 2:
An interview template

1 Think of a job and write an interview questionnaire. Then interview your partner for the job.

Interview questionnaire

Name: _____

Occupation: _____

_____
_____
_____
_____
_____
_____
_____
_____
_____
_____
_____
_____
_____
_____
_____
_____
_____
_____
_____

2 Write three top tips for anyone going to an interview.

1 _____
2 _____
3 _____

7 It's the law!

Vocabulary 1

Using the worksheet

- This worksheet provides practice of the core words: *judge, detective, reporter, cameraman, crime, criminal, headline, interview, article.*

1 Learners work in pairs to complete the crossword. Fast finishers can write sentences in their notebooks.

> Key: **Across** 2 cameraman 3 crime 4 headline 6 reporter 8 article
> **Down** 1 criminal 5 detective 7 interview

2 Learners work in pairs and use the code to complete the words in the text.

> Key: 1 detective, 2 crime, 3 criminal, 4 interviewed, 5 judge

Optional follow-up activity (reinforcement):
Play 'Vocabulary Ladders'. Divide the class into two teams. Each team lines up at the board. Draw a column for team A and one for team B. When you say *Go!* Learners take turns to write as many words as they can from the vocabulary set. Each learner has to write a different word. The first team to finish wins.

Grammar 1

Using the worksheet

- This worksheet provides practice of the target language of reported speech.

1 Learners write the equivalent reported speech expressions.

> Key: 1 the previous week, 2 then, 3 the previous year, 4 the day before, 5 that, 6 the following day 7 those, 8 there

2 Learners circle the words that will change in the report. Fast finishers can write the underlined words as reported speech.

> Key: Kelly: Help! There's a burglar in a house. I saw the same man in the neighbourhood <u>last week</u>.
> Police: Where are you?
> Kelly: I'<u>m standing</u> outside my neighbour's house and I'<u>ve</u> just <u>seen</u> a man with their TV and laptop.
> Police: What's the address?
> Kelly: It's 94 Grange Road.
> Police: Ok Can you see the man now?
> Kelly: Yes he just <u>ran</u> into the park.
> Police: What was he wearing?
> Kelly: He'<u>s wearing</u> a black tracksuit and trainers.
> Police: OK. We are coming.
> Kelly: All right. I <u>will</u> check if he <u>is</u> still in the park.
> Police: No, just stay where you are.
> Kelly: OK. I'll stay here.

3 Learners work in pairs. They take turns to report what their witnesses have said to each other. Fast finishers can write up a police report on what the witnesses said.

> Key: Suggested answers
> Student A: Witness 1 said a woman was standing outside the bank. Witness 2 said there had been four men dressed as clowns. Witness 3 said he said he could see the clowns, they were riding away on motorbikes. Student B: Witness 4 said they were carrying bags full of money. Witness 5 said she had seen the motorcycles outside an old farm house. Witness 6 said four men had come out of the farmhouse and they had driven away in a red car.

Optional follow-up activity (extension):
Ask learners work in small groups of four. Make a list of people that learners will have spoken to in their lives, e.g. *parent, brother/sister, teacher, friend, grandparent, neighbour.* Write these on the board. Ask learners to choose one of the people on the board and think of something they have said to them. They don't tell their partner who it is. They report back two or three sentences that the person said to them to their group and the group has to guess who the person is.

Vocabulary 2

Using the worksheet

- This worksheet provides practice of the core vocabulary: *interrupted, screaming, suggested, whispered, asked, demanded, joked, complained, claimed, replied.*

1 Learners read the sentences and write T or F. Fast finishers can correct the wrong sentences.

> Key: 1 T, 2 F, 3 T, 4 T, 5 F, 6 F, 7 T, 8 F

2 Learners complete the sentences in pairs.

> Key: 1 suggested, 2 screaming, 3 whispered, 4 replied, 5 demanded, 6 asked, 7 complained, 8 claimed

3 Learners work in pairs. They cut out the cards and place them in a pile face down. They take turns to take a card and say what kind of reporting verb it is.

> Key: 1 suggest, 2 ask, 3 claim, 4 reply, 5 demand, 6 complain, 7 whisper, 8 joked, 9 reply

Optional follow-up activity (reinforcement):
Divide the class into two teams. Invite a member from each team to the front and whisper one of the reporting verbs in their ear. The team member has to say a statement, which explains the word without saying it for their team to guess.

Grammar 2

Using the worksheet

- This worksheet provides practice of reported questions.

1 Learners circle the correct option.

> Key: 1 why I was, 2 had seen, 3 I would interview, 4 I could, 5 I knew

2 Learners rewrite the questions as reported questions.

> Key: 1 Molly asked Jack where Tiger was. 2 Molly asked Jack if he thought someone had stolen Tiger. 3 Molly asked if Jack could help her look for Tiger. 4 Molly asked Jack what she should do if she couldn't find Tiger. 5 Molly asked Jack if he would help her make some posters.

3 Learners work in pairs and read the speech bubbles.

> Key: 1 They asked him why he had stolen the TV. 2 They asked me what time I had seen the man leave the house. 3 He asked if I knew what kind of car he had driven. 4 He asked where I had been the previous night at 9.p.m. 5 He asked who I had been with.

Optional follow-up activity (reinforcement):
Ask learners to sit in a circle. Start by whispering something in a learner's ear, e.g. *Can you bake a cake?* The learner then has to report what question you asked until the last learner who must say the original question.

Skills 1: Listening and speaking

Using the worksheet

- This worksheet provides listening and speaking skills practice linked to the unit topic of the law. The listening skill is listening for specific information.

1 Learners listen to a reporter talk about his career. Play the audio and ask learners a gist question, e.g. *How does Eric feel about his job?* He liked it. Play the audio again, pausing for learners to write.

> Key: 1 The Echo Times, 2 1986, 3 tea and coffee, 4 wedding ring, 5 right questions 6 the story

Track 07
Teacher: Today let's welcome Mr Eric Brown to our class. He's a reporter from Channel 4 News.
Eric Thank you very much. When I finished high school I didn't go to university. I started working at a small newspaper called *The Echo Times*. That was in 1986. I didn't actually do much reporting. I was mostly making tea and coffee and doing chores for the real reporters. Sometimes I went with a reporter out on jobs. That was really exciting. After three years I was promoted – I was finally a crime reporter. I remember the first person I interviewed. I went with my cameraman to the address. It was a lady. Her wedding ring had been stolen. She claimed to have heard a strange noise in her house the previous week. She said she had screamed and called the police but when they looked there was no one there. She said she hadn't used her ring for years because it was damaged, one of the diamonds had fallen out were missing because she was going to a party that night. I asked if she lived alone. She said she lived with her husband but he was away on a business trip. The following day her husband returned from his trip and presented her with her wedding ring. He had taken it on his trip and had the diamond replaced! That experience taught me how important it is to ask the right questions during an interview. The funniest case I ever reported on was a case of a criminal who was hiding from police. As the police were searching the building they were about to give up and then the police officer shouted 'Marco!' A few minutes later the thief had replied 'Polo!' Even the judge started laughing at that one. I really enjoy going to court because you hear both sides of the story.

2 Learners work in pairs and describe what they can see in the photos.
3 Learners ask and answer the questions. Ask a few pairs to share their ideas with the class.

Optional follow-up activity (extension):
Play the audio again. Write a few statements on the board and ask learners to say if they are true or false.

Skills 2: Reading and writing

Using the worksheet

- This worksheet provides reading and writing skills practice in understanding a text about jobs and careers.

1 Learners read the text. Ask learners what they think of the text and which prison they think is the most interesting. They can work in pairs to do the activity.

> Key: 1 C, 2 F, 3 E, 4 B, 5 G

61

7 Vocabulary 1

Across
2. a person who films people in a court
3. an action that breaks the law
4. this appears at the top of a newspaper and is a brief description of the topic
6. a type of journalist
8. a piece of text about something which appears in a newspaper

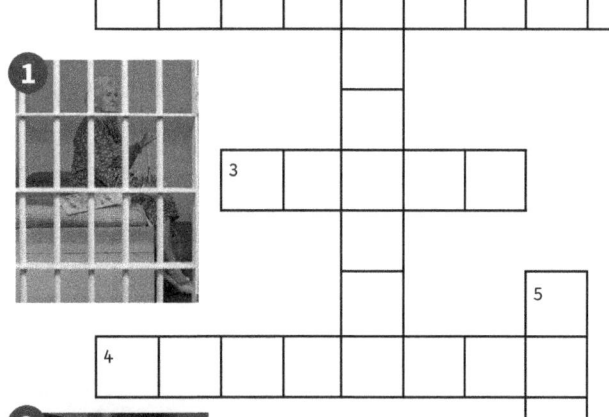

Down
1. A person that breaks the law
5. a police officer that investigates a crime
7. this happens when a police officer asks a criminal questions about a crime

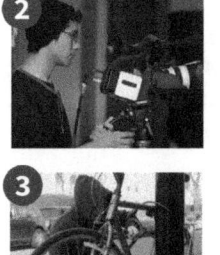

1 Use the clues to complete the puzzle.

2 Use the code to complete the newspaper article.

A	B	C	D	E	F	G	H	I	J	K	L	M
%	@	546	^	&	213	$	987	£	989	+	132	=
N	O	P	Q	R	S	T	U	V	W	X	Y	Z
794	-	937	?	303	>	639	<	|	748	121	809	312

A pet shop on Oxford Street was burgled late last night. The **(1)** ^ & 639 & 546 639 £ | & _____ investigating the **(2)** 546 303 £ = & _____ said it was a mystery where all the animals went to. After following up some clues he discovered some of the missing animals at an address in Seymour Grove. The **(3)** 546 303 £ = £ 794 % 132 _____ had put an advert in front of his home, which read 'Pets for Sale'. There was a long queue of parents and children outside the home. The man was arrested and sent to jail. When he was **(4)** £ 794 639 & 303 | £ & 748 & ^ _____ by the police, he said he wanted to make some extra money. As punishment the **(5)** 989 < ^ $ & _____ ordered the man to work in the local zoo for one month – cleaning out the animals' homes.

7 Grammar 1

1 Write reported speech sentences using the following direct speech expressions.

1 two days ago _____
2 now _____
3 last year _____
4 yesterday _____
5 this _____
6 tomorrow _____
7 these _____
8 here _____

2 Read the dialogue. Imagine Kelly is telling her friend about what she told the police officer the next day. Circle the words that Kelly says that would have to be changed when she reports it to her friend.

Kelly: Help! There's a burglar in a house. I saw the same man in the neighbourhood last week.

Police: Where are you?

Kelly: I'm standing outside my neighbour's house and I've just seen a man with their TV and laptop.

Police: What's the address?

Kelly: It's 94 Grange Road.

Police: OK. Can you see the man now?

Kelly: Yes, he just ran into the park.

Police: What was he wearing?

Kelly: He's wearing a black tracksuit and trainers.

Police: OK. We are coming.

Kelly: All right. I will check if he is still in the park.

Police: No, just stay where you are.

Kelly: OK. I'll stay here.

3 Work in pairs. Cut out the cards. Imagine you are a detectives and you have interviewed people who saw a bank robbery taking place. Read the notes and then take turns to tell your partner what the witnesses said.

Learner A
Witness 1: A woman is standing outside the bank.
Witness 2: There were four men dressed as clowns inside the bank.
Witness 3: I can see the clowns, they are riding away on motorbikes.

Learner B
Witness 4: They are carrying bags full of money.
Witness 5: I saw the motorcycles outside an old farmhouse.
Witness 6. Four men came out of the farmhouse and drove away in a red car.

7 Vocabulary 2

1 Read the sentences and write T (True) or F (False). Correct the false statements and write them in your notebooks.

1 When you say something as a question you ask. _____
2 When you make a loud noise because you are scared you complain. _____
3 When you make a strong request you demand. _____
4 When you answer a question you reply. _____
5 When you say something for other people to think about you joke. _____
6 When you speak in a low voice you claim. _____
7 When you stop someone when they are doing or saying something you interrupt. _____
8 When you say something to make others laugh you whisper. _____

2 Complete the sentences with the correct words. The first letter of each word has been given to you.

1 'Let's interview the criminal at 3 p.m.' Alex s_____.
2 I heard s_____ coming from the house last night.
3 Helen w_____ in my ear, 'I forgot to bring my passport.'
4 'The judge sentenced him to 10 years in prison,' Jack r_____.
5 'What did you do with my phone?' David d_____.
6 'Why did you commit the crime?' the detective a_____ the criminal.
7 'There's too much work to do. We'll never finish it!' Lisa c_____.
8 'I know who stole the teddy bear,' Hannah c_____.

3 Work in pairs. Cut out the cards. Take turns to read the sentence on the card and report it using a reporting verb.

1 You should go to the police.	2 What did the judge say?	3 I saw the robbers.
4 Because I fell off my bike.	5 What have you done?	6 Jack hasn't done the washing up again.
7 Don't make any noise. The burglars are still in the house.	8 The mouse chased the cat out of the garden!	9 Because I didn't sleep last night.

7 Grammar 2

1 **Circle the correct text.**
1. She asked me *why I was/why was I* late.
2. He asked me if I *did see/had seen* the headline.
3. She asked me whether *would I interview/ I would interview* the criminal.
4. He asked me whether *could I / I could* drive.
5. She asked me if *I knew / I did* know the judge.

2 **Read the dialogue and write the reported questions on the lines.**

Molly: Where is Tiger? **(1)** _____

Jack: I don't know. I haven't seen him for a while.

Molly: Do you think someone has stolen him? **(2)** _____

Jack: I don't think so. Maybe he's just gone for a walk around the neighbourhood.

Molly: Can you help me look for him? **(3)** _____

Jack: Yes, of course.

Molly: What should I do if I can't find him? **(4)** _____

Jack: I suggest you make some posters of him with his picture and stick them up around the neighbourhood. I'm sure someone has seen him.

Molly: Good idea. Will you help me make some posters? **(5)** _____

Jack: Of course. But first let's go and look for him.

3 **Work in pairs. Look at the speech bubbles and say what questions the people asked using reported speech.**

- Why did you steal the TV?
- What time did you see the man leave the house?
- Do you know what kind of car he was driving?
- Where were you last night at 9 p.m.?
- Who were you with?

7 Skills 1: Listening and speaking

1 🎧 07 **For each question, write the correct answer in the gap. Write one or two words or a number or a date or a time.**

1 Eric's first job after high school was at a newspaper called _____.
2 He started working there in _____.
3 At that time he said his job involved making _____ and doing chores.
4 The first person he interviewed was a lady who said her _____ had been stolen.
5 He said the experience had taught him that it was important to ask the _____.
6 He said he enjoyed going to court because he heard both sides of _____.

2 Work with a partner. Say what you can see in the pictures.

In this picture I can see…   I can also see …

3 Work with a partner. Ask and answer the questions.

1 Would you like to do any of the jobs shown in the pictures?
2 Do you think these jobs are important? Why? Why not?
3 Why do you think criminals commit crimes?
4 Do you think all criminals should go to prison?
5 How do you think we could reduce crime?

7 Skills 2: Reading and writing

Five sentences have been removed from the article. Choose from the sentences (A–H) to fill each gap (1–5). There are three extra sentences.

Unusual prisons around the world

In India there is a special kind of prison. Yerwada Prison is unique.
(1) _____
The prison director said that yoga improved mental and physical health. It made the prisoners feel calm and less likely to commit more crimes.
(2) _____
The prison director claimed that the yoga course has resulted in less bad behaviour within the prison.

Zomba Prison in Malawi became famous in 2016 when the prisoners won a Grammy award for their album. Prisoners and guards complained the prison was a very difficult place to live and work. It was built for 400 prisoners but today there are over 2000 prisoners. But when you walk into this crowded place, the first thing you hear is music. Prisoners and guards perform together. The idea was started by a prison guard, Thomas Binamo. (3) _____
He said at first there had been only a few prisoners interested. Then, as more prisoners heard the sounds of music coming from the yard they joined in. When asked how music has helped him, one of the prisoners replied that music took him to another place – it was like escaping.

There are over 1000 prisoners at Cebu Prison in the Philippines. It is famous for its dancing prisoners. (4) _____
_____ The prison director said that dance helped to reduce problems with criminals and made them more ready for release into society. By working to together as a team, he said they learnt important skills for the outside world. The prisoners' most famous performance was of Michael Jackson's 'Thriller' dance. (5) _____
_____
The prisoner's dance moves have made headlines around the world and reporters have come to the prison to interview them. They have even taken part in dance festivals!

A   There is a library for prisoners.
B   Prisoners spend up to four hours a day practising dance moves.
C   If they pass a yoga course than can be released from the prison early.
D   They can also do courses in maths, English and other subjects.
E   He said he had started a band in the prison in 2008.
F   Prisoners who take the course are encouraged to teach yoga to prisoners in other prisons around India.
G   A video of the dance performance was uploaded to YouTube and viewed more than 10 million times.
H   They cook their own meals.

7 Mission Final Stage: A news website

Write an article about an incident for a news website. Draw a picture where the photo would be.

Daily News

Title

8 Fantastic flavours

Vocabulary 1

Using the worksheet

- This worksheet provides practice of the core words: *starter, main course, dessert, tuna, rice, cucumber, coconut, cream, curry, pear, spinach.*
1 Learners work in pairs to match the two parts of the words. Then label the pictures.

> Key: 1 d, 2 e, 3 f, 4 k, 5 g, 6 c, 7 j, 8 b, 9 a, 10 h
> Pictures: 1 curry 2 coconut 3 cream 4 rice 5 dessert 6 cucumber 7 spinach 8 tuna 9 pear 10 starter

2 Learners complete the menu individually.

> Key: 1 Starter, 2 cucumber, 3 Main course, 4 coconut, 5 tuna, 6 cream

Optional follow-up activity (reinforcement):
Learners work in pairs. They take turns to describe a food item to their partner without saying the word. You could brainstorm adjectives to describe food with learners and write them on the board, e.g. *healthy, tasty, soft, hard, spicy*. Then demonstrate the activity with one food item. Give three clues for learners to guess the item.

Grammar 1

Using the worksheet

- This worksheet provides practice of the target language of reflexive pronouns.
1 Learners correct the mistakes in the sentences.

> Key: 1 (I myself cooked) I cooked myself
> 2 (themselves) herself, 3 (itself) himself, 4 (ourself) ourselves, 5 (yourself) myself

2 This is a mingling activity. Learners walk around the classroom asking the questions. They write down the name of the learner and a sentence with their reply using reflexive pronouns.

Optional follow-up activity (extension):
You could extend the above questionnaire by asking learners to think of three more questions to add to the survey. They can then ask their partner the questions and write down the answers. Invite pairs to share their questions with the class. You could also do a quick survey based on the questions from Activity 2.

Vocabulary 2

Using the worksheet

- This worksheet provides practice of the core vocabulary: *tasty, awful, disgusting, sweet, bitter, fantastic, flavour, healthy, fresh, spicy.*
1 Learners find and circle the words in the circles. They then use the words to complete the sentences.

> Key: 1 awful, 2 tasty, 3 fresh, 4 sweet, 5 spicy, 6 fantastic, 7 flavour, 8 disgusting

2 Learners circle the correct words in the text.

> Key: 1 healthy, 2 fresh, 3 tasty, 4 spicy, 5 sweet

Optional follow-up activity (reinforcement):
Divide the class into groups of three or four. Ask each group to make word cards with all the words from this vocabulary set: *tasty, awful, disgusting, sweet, bitter, fantastic, flavour, healthy, fresh, amazing*. Each group arranges all the cards face up on the table and studies each card's position on the table. You could use your mobile phone to time this for 1 minute. Then instruct learners to turn over the cards face down. Learners take turns try and remember the position of each card. They do this by choosing a card to describe and then turning the card over. If their description matches the word they keep the card. If not they put the card face down in the same position. You could demonstrate the game with a group. Ask the class to gather round. Choose a card that you know what the word is, give the definition and turn it over. If the definition matches explain that you can keep the card. The winner is the learner with the most cards at the end.

Grammar 2

Using the worksheet

- This worksheet provides practice of the target language of *enough/too* and *for/to*.
1 Learners complete the text with *too/enough* and *for/to*.

> Key: 1 enough, 2 for, 3 too, 4 to, 5 too, 6 for

2 Learners work in pairs and invent answers for the questions using enough/too and for/to. Ask some pairs to share their answers with the class.

> **Key: Suggested answers** 1 Because it was too spicy for me to eat. 2 No, because we weren't strong enough to break the shell. 3 No, insects are too disgusting for me to eat. 4 She prefers it cooked because fresh spinach isn't tasty enough for her. 5 No, it was too cold for me to swim.

3 Learners work in pairs and describe the pictures.

> **Key: Suggested answers** 1 There isn't enough food to make lunch. 2 The shoes are too big for her. 3 The train is too crowded today. 4 The pan isn't big enough to fry that fish.

Optional follow-up activity (reinforcement):
Divide the class into four teams. Assign each team a number and a space on the board to write. Each team has to nominate a writer. The writers stand at their space on the board. Each team then nominates a runner – the person who runs to the board. If running isn't an option, learners can walk to the board. Give each team a different key word, e.g. *big, small, hot, cold, bitter, sweet, tasty, disgusting*. Then each team must make a sentence with the keyword and either *enough/too* and *for/to*. The runner must run or walk to the board and tell the writer the sentence for them to write.

Skills 1: Listening and speaking

Using the worksheet
- This worksheet provides listening and speaking skills practice linked to the unit topic of food. The listening skill is listening for specific information.

1 Learners listen to the audios. Ask gist questions, e.g. 1 *Where are the friends?* In a restaurant 2 *What are the friends planning?* What to cook 3 *Where are they?* In a market

> **Key:** 1 C, 2 B, 4 A, 5 C, 6 A

Track 8
Wendy: What are you going to have for your starter?
Jack: I'll have the cheese salad, and for my main course I'll have the curry.
Wendy: Nice. I made myself a curry last week but it wasn't spicy enough for me. For my main course I can't decide between the chicken with potatoes or the tuna with rice and spinach.
Jack: The tuna sounds healthy.
Wendy: Yes, and I eat chicken all the time at home. I'll have the tuna.

Jessica: What shall we cook tonight?
Peter: What about a curry?
Jessica: Good idea but we haven't got enough chilli or rice.
Peter: I don't like my curry too spicy. I'll just get some rice from the supermarket.

Jessica: Great. And we have some chicken in the fridge we can put in the curry sauce.

Jane: What is that? It smells disgusting!
Billy: It's called durian fruit. It's a type of fruit in Thailand.
Jane: The skin is spiky.
Billy: Yes. In Thailand people use it to add flavour to many different types of dishes.
Jane: These apples smell delicious and they are so big. Shall we buy some?
Billy: Good idea! Let's go and look at the vegetables.

Helen: Can you cook anything for yourself?
Alex: I can cook myself an omelette with tuna. What about you?
Helen: I can make desserts like cakes. I'm not very good with main courses. Whenever I try to make them they aren't tasty enough to eat. My mum makes delicious potatoes and chicken. She cooks them in the oven.

David: I really want to learn to make nice desserts but anything I try to make is awful.
Molly: Why don't you try reading this cooking blog… it's really good and has lots of helpful tips.
David: My sister suggested I do a course and practise making simple cakes, but, yeah, I think I'll start with that blog.

Adam: How was your cooking course?
Teresa: It was fantastic. I really enjoyed it. It was hard in the beginning because I didn't know anything about cooking. And most people were much older than me, but everyone was so friendly and nice in the end.

2 Learners work in pairs and describe what they can see in the photos.

3 Learners ask and answer the questions. Ask a few pairs to share their ideas with the class.

Optional follow-up activity (extension):
Ask learners to design their ideal meal, including a starter, main course and dessert.

Skills 2: Reading and writing

Using the worksheet
- This worksheet provides reading and writing skills practice in understanding a text about food.

1 Learners read the text. Ask learners what they think of the text. They can work in pairs to do the activity.

> **Key:** 1 A, 2 C, 3 D, 4 D, 5 C, 6 C

2 Learners write about an unusual dish from their country. They can use the Internet to do research and add photos to their notes.

3 Learners compare the dish they wrote about with the ones mentioned in Activity 1.

8 Vocabulary 1

1 Match the two parts of the words. Then write the words under the correct picture.

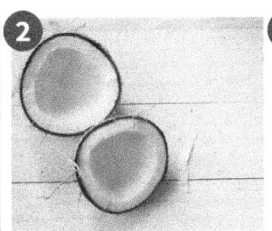

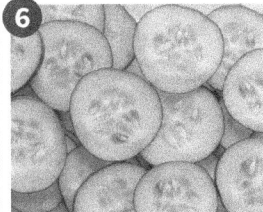

1	star	a	ber
2	cre	b	sert
3	pe	c	nut
4	ri	d	ter
5	spi	e	am
6	coco	f	ry
7	cur	g	nach
8	des	h	na
9	cucum	i	ar
10	tu	j	ce

2 Complete the menus with the correct words from the box.

coconut   Main course   Starter   cucumber   cream   tuna

Small World *restaurant menu*

(1) _____

Vegetable tempura: deep-fried crispy mix of vegetables in tempura batter served with sweet chilli dip.

Greek salad: slices of tomatoes, onions, peppers, (2) _____ with feta cheese and black olives.

Prosciutto e melone: cubes of melon wrapped in Italian Parma ham.

(3) _____

Meat

Chicken cooked in Thailand's classic mild hot sauce, which is a mix of many ingredients like curry, garlic, red chillies, sugar and (4) _____ milk.

Cheese burger: 100% British beef burger and cheddar cheese, served with chips.

Fish

Roast swordfish served with fresh leaves of spinach and rocket.

Grilled (5) _____ served with rice and boiled vegetables.

Dessert

Pear tart: Granny's homemade pear tart.

Belgian chocolate cake served with (6) _____.

8 Grammar 1

1 Find the mistakes in the sentences. Write the correct sentences on the lines.

1 Yesterday I myself cooked roast potatoes without asking my older sister for help!
   _____

2 My mum is great, for Christmas she is going to cook two starters, three main courses with lamb, turkey and beef, and a couple of desserts – all that themselves!
   _____

3 I remember when Paul was four years old he was able to peel a pear itself.
   _____

4 The wardrobe in the bedroom corner is 30 years old; my dad and I built it yourself.
   _____

5 I didn't manage to make a good vegetable curry yourself, even after watching a video online.
   _____

2 Ask your classmates the following questions. Write their names in the chart. Write a sentence about each learner's answer.

Student A: Maria, what food can you make yourself?

Student B: I can make a cake myself.

Sentence: Maria can make a cake herself.

Question	Student name	Sentence
What's the most difficult main course your mum can make herself?		
Did you ever hurt yourself in the kitchen?		
Can you make a chocolate cake yourself?		
Has your brother or sister ever cooked a dish by himself/herself?		
Do you know people who can cut their hair themselves?		
Does you mum enjoy herself when she watches football?		
How many times a day do you look at yourself in the mirror?		
Have you ever cooked a meal for yourself?		
Have your best friends ever opened a coconut themselves?		

8 Vocabulary 2

1 Circle the words in the word snake. Then complete the sentences with the words.

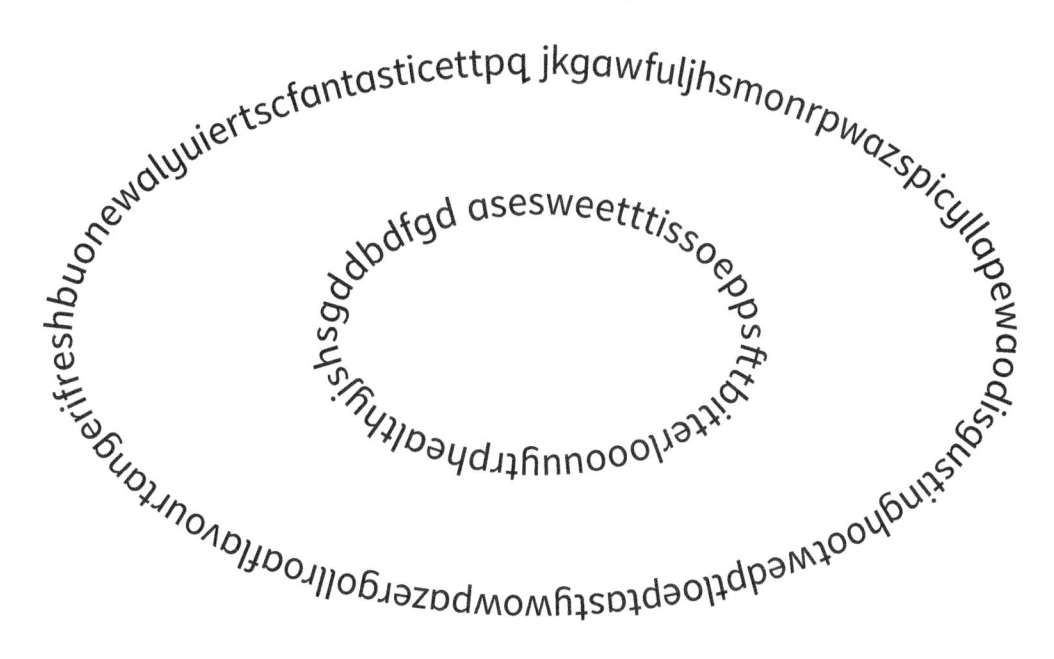

1 The food I made myself was _____. I couldn't eat it.
2 Curry is _____ because it has a lot of different ingredients and spices in it.
3 A lot of Asian dishes mix cooked and _____ ingredients in the same dish.
4 Do you prefer your coffee _____ or bitter?
5 In cold countries food is not traditionally _____ because chilli peppers and other hot spices don't grow there.
6 My mum always cooks _____ pasta and rice dishes. She is a great cook.
7 Her favourite ice cream _____ is coconut.
8 Did you ever try raw meat? Some people find it _____, but some people like it.

2 Read the text. Circle the correct words to complete the sentences.

My name is Sarah. I'm half British, half Thai, I was born and grew up in Birmingham. My father is English and my mother comes from Thailand. My mum works as a doctor in a hospital and is often too busy to cook, so my grandmother cooks most of the time. She is Thai. Thai food is my favourite food. I love it because they manage to make **(1) healthy/disgusting** food by using very different ingredients and flavours. For example, my grandma makes a curry with fish and on the top she adds some **(2) bitter/fresh** herbs like coriander, parsley or mint. Often she uses coconut milk in very hot dishes, so it turns out very **(3) awful/tasty** and at the same time **(4) spicy/flavour** and **(5) sweet/bitter**.

8 Grammar 2

1 Complete the text with *too/enough* and *for/to*.

Last weekend I went to Mary's birthday party, but when I arrived I thought to myself, I don't know **(1)** _____ people here, I'd better go home. As I was about to leave, a girl started talking to me – she's called Anna. We started talking and discovered we had a lot in common.

At some point, Mary cut the cake, but there wasn't enough **(2)** _____ everyone, so Anna shared her piece with me. We both agreed the cake was **(3)** _____ sweet for us **(4)** _____ eat. Then some boys put on some music. It was **(5)** _____ loud **(6)** _____ us to talk, so we went out to the garden and carried on talking.

After a fun afternoon laughing and getting to know each other she left, but she gave me her phone number and we are going to meet up again. So in the end it didn't matter that I didn't know many people at the party because I made a new friend!

2 Invent answers to the questions using *too/enough* and *for/to*.

1 Why didn't you eat the curry?
   _____

2 Did you have the coconut Grandpa bought from the market?
   _____

3 Have you ever eaten fried insects?
   _____

4 How does your mum like spinach, fresh or cooked?
   _____

5 Did you go swimming in the sea?
   _____

3 Work in pairs. Describe for the pictures using *enough, too ... for/to*.

74 Power Up TRB 6 © Cambridge University Press and UCLES 2018 **PHOTOCOPIABLE**

8 Skills 1: Listening and speaking

1 🎧 **For each question, choose the correct answer.**

1 You will hear two friends talking about what to eat. What does the girl decide to have?
   A a curry
   B chicken and potatoes
   C tuna with rice and spinach

2 You will hear two friends talking about what they need. What does the boy agree to buy?
   A chilli
   B rice
   C chicken

3 You will hear two friends discussing fruit. What does the girl dislike about the durian fruit?
   A the smell
   B the size
   C how it feels

4 You will hear two friends talking about cooking. What can the boy cook for himself?
   A desserts
   B chicken with potatoes
   C omelette with tuna

5 You will hear two friends talking about learning to cook. What does the girl advise the boy to do?
   A make simple cakes
   B do a course
   C read a blog

6 You will hear two friends talking about a cooking course. How did the girl feel about her course?
   A she thought it was fantastic
   B she thought it was too difficult
   C she thought she wasn't old enough for the class

2 **Work with a partner. Say what you can see in the pictures.**

> In this picture I can see...

> I can also see...

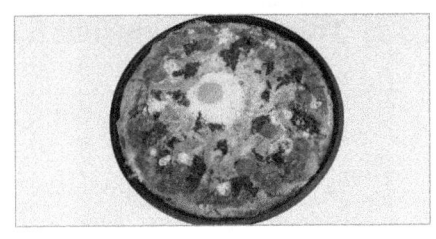

3 **Work with a partner. Ask and answer the questions.**

1 Which foods do you like in the pictures?
2 Which of the pictures show a main course?
3 Which of the pictures show starters?
4 Which are desserts?
5 Which do you think is the most tasty?
6 Which do you think is the most spicy?

PHOTOCOPIABLE   Power Up TRB 6 © Cambridge University Press and UCLES 2018   75

8 Skills 2: Reading and writing

1 Read the text below and choose the correct word for each space. For each question, mark A, B, C or D next to the correct word.

Unusual food from around the world

The food we love very much depends on where we come from. A dish that one person finds **tasty** could be (1) _____ to another person. Here are a few of the most unusual (or most normal) foods from around the world.

Fugu

In Japan you can have this as a (2) _____ before your main meal. It's called puffer fish. If humans eat the fish it is very dangerous because it has something inside it that can kill us. Chefs in Japan train for several years before they can prepare it (3) _____. When it is cooked the fish doesn't have much (4) _____ but it is the danger of eating it that attracts so many people.

Brain sandwiches

If Fugu isn't unusual (5) _____ you, then why not try a brain sandwich? These come from the USA. In Ohio you can get fried brain sandwiches.

Insects

In Cambodia fried tarantula spiders are considered a very special treat. In parts of Africa many people eat barbecued crickets, ants, worms and grasshoppers. Insects are a healthy food because they contain vitamins which are good for our bodies. However, for some people, insects are just too awful (6) _____ eat!

1	A disgusting	B fresh	C healthy	D sweet
2	A main course	B dessert	C starter	D snack
3	A ourselves	B yourselves	C himself	D themselves
4	A fresh	B bitter	C fantastic	D flavour
5	A enough to	B too for	C enough for	D too to
6	A for	B on	C to	D in

2 Think of an unusual food from your country. Write your answers.
1 What is it called? _____
2 What is it made of? _____
3 Is it a starter, main course or dessert? _____
4 What does it taste like? _____
5 Do you like it? Why? Why not? _____

3 Compare the food in your country with the food mentioned in the text.
_____
_____
_____
_____

8 Mission Stages 1 and 2: A restaurant menu

1 Plan a menu for a new café.

❦ Menu ❧

Starter

Main course

Dessert

2 Write a description of each dish.

_____
_____
_____
_____
_____
_____
_____
_____
_____
_____

9 Raining cats and dogs

Vocabulary 1

Using the worksheet

- This worksheet provides practice of the core words: *weather forecast, degrees, snowfall, breeze, shower, sunshine, heat, gales, thunder, lighting, temperature, storm*.

1 Learners work in pairs and circle the words in the word search. Then they write the words next to the correct pictures.

> Key: 1 forecast, 2 degrees, 3 snowfall, 4 gales, 5 breeze, 6 shower, 7 temperature, 8 storm, 9 sunshine, 10 thunder, 11 lightning, 12 thermometer

2 Learners complete the text individually. Fast finishers can write sentences with the words in their notebooks.

> Key: 1 storm, 2 sunshine, 3 degrees, 4 shower, 5 gales, 6 snowfall

Optional follow-up activity (reinforcement):
Make A4 word cards for the vocabulary set on the classroom walls. Divide the class into two teams and invite a player from each team to the front of the class. Describe a word and the team members have to race to touch the word. The first to touch the word gains a point.

Grammar 1

Using the worksheet

- This worksheet provides practice of the target language of first and second conditionals.

1 Divide learners into groups of four. Each group has two teams. Ensure learners have coloured pencils. Each team chooses a colour. Explain that each team takes turns to choose a number on the board and then make a conditional sentence from the prompts with the same number. When they make a correct sentence, the team can colour in that hexagon. The aim of the game is to colour in a diagonal row across or a column of hexagons without being blocked by the other team.

> Key: 1 If it is sunny tomorrow we won't stay at home. 2 If you saw a tiger what would you do? 3 If it snows at the weekend it will be dangerous to drive. 4 What would you do if you could fly? 5 We will wear T-shirts if it is sunny in Spain. 6 If Beth isn't sick she will have a picnic today with her friends. 7 If there was a light breeze walking to the beach would be more pleasant. 8 They would travel all the time if they didn't have to work. 9 What would you do if you won the competition? 10 If there is a storm the boat won't leave. 11 If I were rich I would plant millions of trees. 12 If the temperature is above 25 degrees we will go swimming on Saturday. 13 She will get sunburn, if she doesn't put on sunscreen. 14 Will you help me if you have time? 15 If you break the thermometer you won't be able to check the temperature. 16 If the weather forecast isn't good we won't go to the beach. 17 If he misses the bus he won't arrive at school on time. 18 What would you do if you lost your mobile phone? 19 I would be happy if I saw a panda bear. 20 They will be disappointed if their team don't win.

Optional follow-up activity (extension):
Ask students to write the first part of three first conditional sentence. Ask learners to cut their sentences halves out, leaving space for the second half of the sentence. Then place them in a bag. Ask learners to take turns to pick a sentence and write the second half. Then invite individuals to read out their sentences. Repeat the process with the second conditional.

Vocabulary 2

Using the worksheet

- This worksheet provides practice of the core vocabulary: *typical, warm, humid, wet, mild, freezing, dry, snowy, icy, cool*.

Learners work in A/B pairs to complete the crossword. They have to ask about and explain words to do so. Cut up the worksheets and give them out. Learners look at their puzzles and at the example. To check that they understand the task, ask stronger learners to do one or two examples in open pairs. In weaker classes, you may like learners to work in A and B groups first to prepare their answers. They can do this orally or take notes, e.g. What's 3 down? Not too hot or too cold. Learners work in A/B pairs to ask, answer and complete their puzzles.

> Key: Learners show each other their worksheet to check their answers.

Optional follow-up activity (reinforcement):
Play 'Write It Up'. Divide the class into teams of four. Give each team a number and write their number on the board, leaving enough space for learners to write sentences. Invite a member from each team to choose a word from the vocabulary set. Each team has to think of a sentence and then a team member must race to the board to write it in their team's space. Teams should check each other's sentences for errors.

Grammar 2
Using the worksheet
- This worksheet provides practice of *I wish*.
1 Learners look at the pictures and guess what the people or animals are wishing for.

> Key: Suggested answers: 1 I wish there wasn't a storm today. 2 I wish I could be a drummer. 3 I wish I could eat the bird. 4 I wish I was a dancer. 5 We wish they didn't cut down the trees.

2 Learners work individually to find and correct the errors in the text.

> Key: I don't (I didn't), he wish (He wishes), could worked (could work), I wished (I wish), I have (I had), I wish

3 Learners draw their wishes then exchange them with their partner who tries to guess the wish and write sentences about them.

Optional follow-up activity (extension):
Extend activity 3. Divide learners into groups of three. Explain to learners that sometimes we have to be careful what we wish for and sometimes if wishes came true they would make lives more difficult. For example, *I wish I was taller. If you were too tall then you wouldn't be able to fit into your favourite clothes.* Explain to learners they are going to take turns to say their wishes and the other members of the group have to imagine something negative happening if their classmate's wish came true. Explain they have to use the second conditional. Demonstrate by writing a wish on the board, e.g. *I wish I was taller.*

Skills 1: Listening and speaking
Using the worksheet
- This worksheet provides listening and speaking skills practice linked to the unit topic of the weather. The listening skill is listening for specific information.
1 Play the audio once for learners to listen. Ask a gist question, e.g. *What has Shirley been invited to the studio to talk about?* Her job.

> Key: 1 C, 2 A, 3 A, 4 A, 5 C, 6 C

Track 09
Presenter: This is ABC Radio 4. Last week we had the journalist Mark Rogers and singer Patty Devine on the programme. This week we are talking about the weather with Shirley Thomas on the programme. She's here to tell us about her long career as a weather woman.
Shirley: Thank you.
Presenter: What made you want to be a weather woman?
Shirley: Well, I studied geography at university. I was always interested in science and the environment. When I finished university I had a few different jobs because I couldn't find a job related to geography. I started working in a shop, then a bank, and finally in
a bookshop. I remember thinking, *I wish I had a more exciting job.* Then after about three years a friend told me about a job on Channel 5. It was presenting the **weather forecast**. I was so happy because
I was so bored with the job I had at the time.
Presenter: What was your first assignment?
Shirley: Oh, my first job was terrible. I was reporting from a **snow storm** on a Welsh mountain. There were severe **gales** and temperatures of about -8 **degrees**. It was **freezing**! I remember thinking at the time, *If I hadn't taken this job I wouldn't be here right now!*
Presenter: Did things improve for you?
Shirley: Well, I had a few difficult days like that. Once I was reporting in the middle of a summer storm in Dorset. There was **thunder** and **lighting** crashing around me. The thunder frightened me the most. I don't mind lightning and wet weather, but the thunder is so loud it shook my body! Another time I reported during heavy **snowfall**. That actually wasn't too bad. I realised that if you don't like getting cold and wet this job isn't for you! It wasn't always bad weather. I often reported on **warm** days with lots of **sunshine**.
Presenter: It sounds like an exciting job.
Shirley: It is. It's hard work and I wish I had more time for my family, but I meet lots of interesting people and I go to amazing places but what I love best about it is that no two days are ever the same.

2 Learners work in pairs and describe what they can see in the photos.

3 Learners ask and answer the questions.

Optional follow-up activity (extension):
Play 'Three Across' with some key words from the audio. Ask learners to draw a grid with nine squares in their notebooks. Write words from the audio on the board: *storm, weather forecast, thunder, warm, freezing, sunshine, lightning, gales, snowfall, degrees.* Ask learners to choose nine words to write in each of their squares. Play the audio and explain when they hear one of the word they have to cross it out. Explain the aim of the game is to cross out words in a row, a column, or diagonally.

Skills 2: Reading and writing
Using the worksheet
- This worksheet provides reading and writing skills practice in understanding a text about the weather in different countries around the world.
1 Learners read the text. Ask what they think.

> Key: 1 H, 2 D, 3 F, 4 A, 5 C

2 Learners write about the weather in their country. They can use the Internet to do research and add photos to their notes.

9 Vocabulary 1

1 Look at the pictures. Find the words in the word square. Then write the words below. The first letter has been given to you.

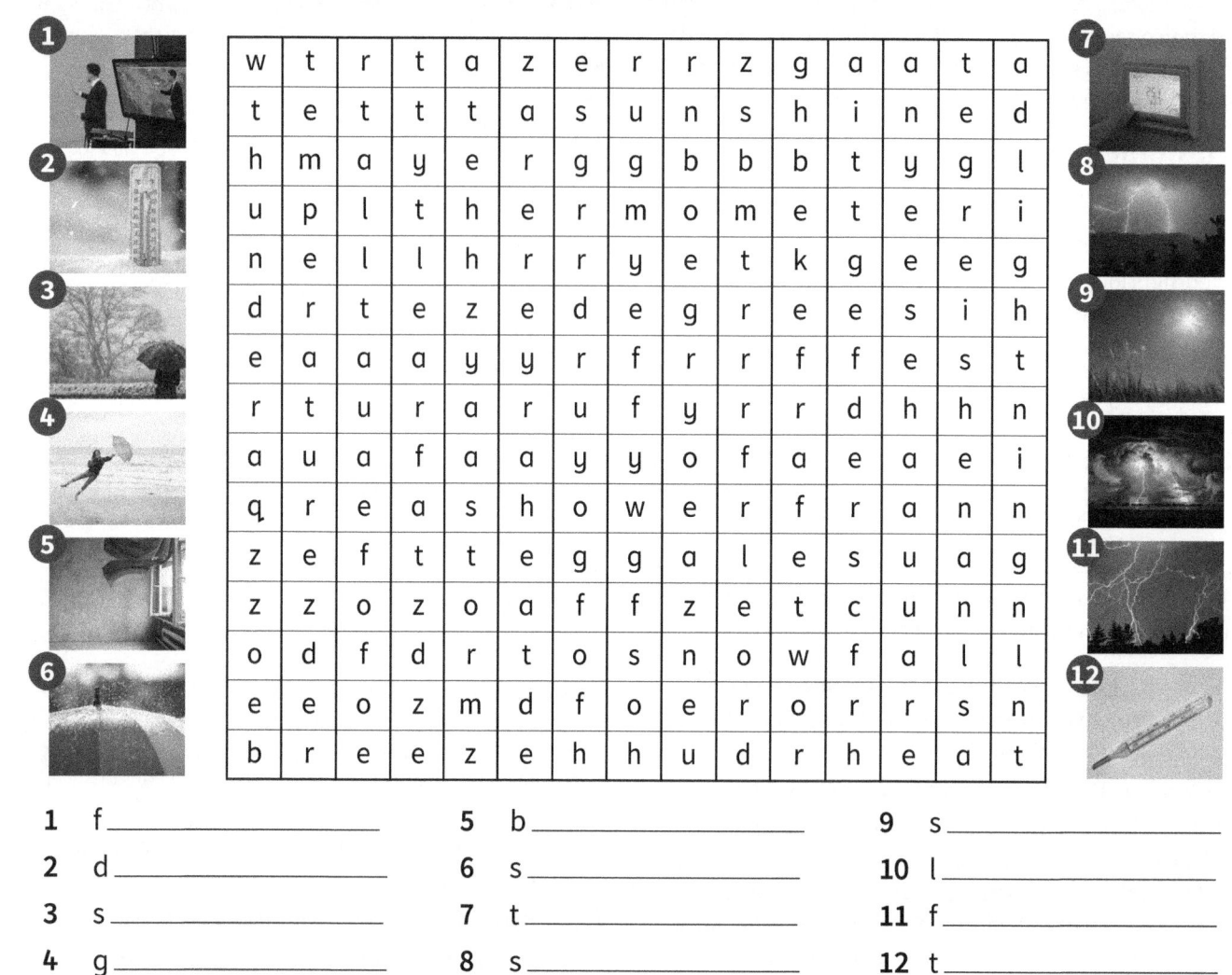

w	t	r	t	a	z	e	r	r	z	g	a	a	t	a
t	e	t	t	a	s	u	n	s	h	i	n	e	d	
h	m	a	y	e	r	g	g	b	b	b	t	y	g	l
u	p	l	t	h	e	r	m	o	m	e	t	e	r	i
n	e	l	l	h	r	r	y	e	t	k	g	e	e	g
d	r	t	e	z	e	d	e	g	r	e	e	s	i	h
e	a	a	a	y	y	r	f	r	r	f	f	e	s	t
r	t	u	r	a	r	u	f	y	r	r	d	h	h	n
a	u	a	f	a	a	y	y	o	f	a	e	a	e	i
q	r	e	a	s	h	o	w	e	r	f	r	a	n	n
z	e	f	t	t	e	g	g	a	l	e	s	u	a	g
z	z	o	z	o	a	f	f	z	e	t	c	u	n	n
o	d	f	d	r	t	o	s	n	o	w	f	a	l	l
e	e	o	z	m	d	f	o	e	r	o	r	r	s	n
b	r	e	e	z	e	h	h	u	d	r	h	e	a	t

1 f_____
2 d_____
3 s_____
4 g_____
5 b_____
6 s_____
7 t_____
8 s_____
9 s_____
10 l_____
11 f_____
12 t_____

2 Complete the online chat with six words from the box.

> breeze   degrees   thunder   snowfall   storm   sunshine   gales   shower

Amanda: Hi Tom! ☺ How is your holiday going in the Amazon?

Tom: Hi Amanda ... There was a scary **1** _____ with strong winds and lots of rain.

Amanda: Really? I'm sorry to hear that. Here we have plenty of **2** _____ and it's very hot. Yesterday my mobile app showed 30 **3** _____, so this morning a light rain **4** _____ was really welcome.

Tom: Here local people say that this kind of extreme weather is not normal, the strong **5** _____ damaged some homes as well. ☹ I guess it's because of global warming. I like it here, though – people are very kind and friendly and I'm learning a lot from them. It never gets very cold here ... imagine that they have never had **6** _____!

80   Power Up TRB 6 © Cambridge University Press and UCLES 2018   **PHOTOCOPIABLE**

9 Grammar 1

1 Read the instructions. Then play the hexagon game.

Instructions
- Play in groups of four. Each pair is a team.
- You need two different coloured pencils.
- Choose a number from the game board and make a conditional sentence from the prompts.
- If you make a correct sentence, colour in the hexagon.
- The aim of the game is for your team to colour in all the hexagons in a diagonal row or in a column from top to bottom without being blocked by the opposite team.

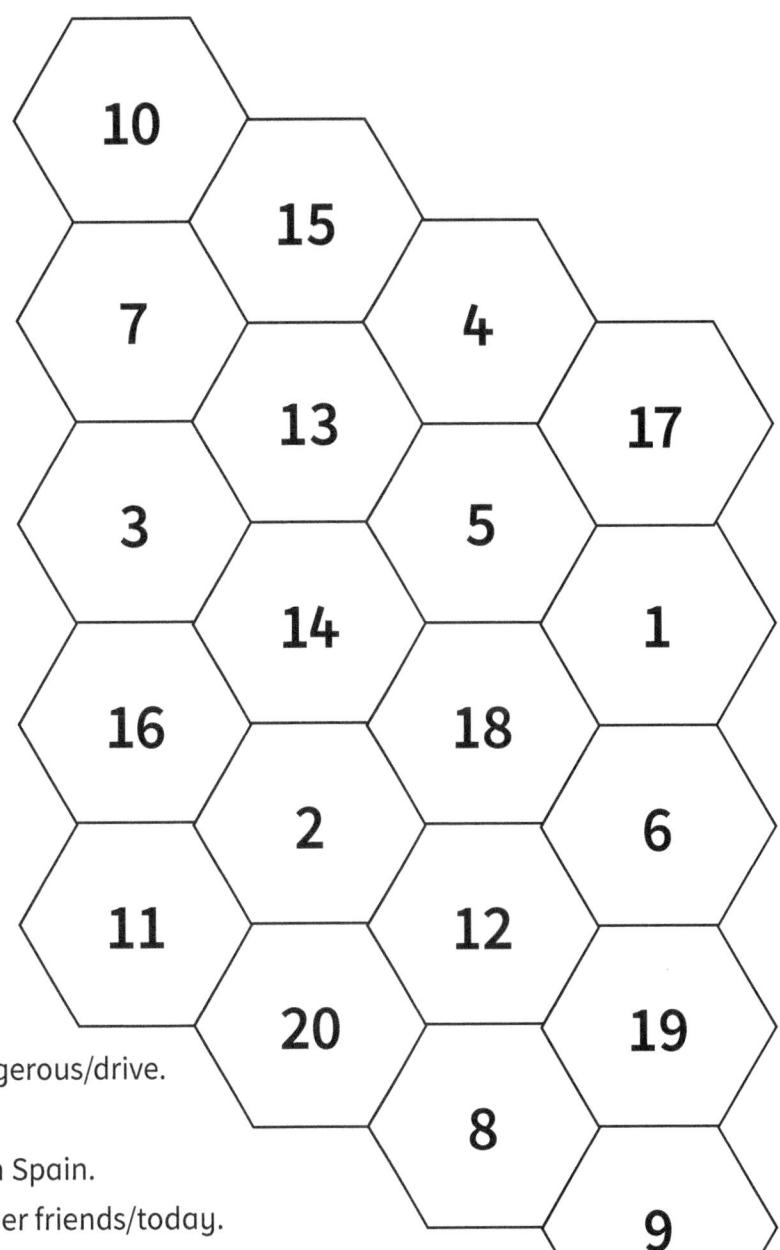

1. if/it/be/sunny/tomorrow/we/not stay/at home.
2. if/you/see/a tiger/what/you/do?
3. if/it/snow/the weekend/it/be/dangerous/drive.
4. what/do/if/you/can/fly?
5. we/wear/T-shirts/if/it/be/sunny/in Spain.
6. if/Beth/not sick/she/have/picnic/her friends/today.
7. if/there/be/a/light breeze/walking/to/the beach/be/more pleasant.
8. they/travel/all the time/if/they/not have to work.
9. what/you/do/win/the/competition?
10. if/there/be/a storm/the boat/not leave.
11. if/I/be/rich/I/plant/millions/trees.
12. if/temperature/be/above/25 degrees/we/go/swimming/on/Saturday.
13. she/get sunburnt/if/she/not put on/sunscreen.
14. you/help/me/if/you/have/time?
15. if/you/break/the thermometer/you/not be/able/to/check/the/temperature.
16. if/the weather forecast/be/not good/we/not go/to the beach.
17. if/he/miss/bus/he/not arrive/at school/on time.
18. what/you/do/if/you/loose/your/mobile phone?
19. I/happy/if/I see/a panda bear.
20. they/be/disappointed/if/their/team/not win.

PHOTOCOPIABLE   Power Up TRB 6 © Cambridge University Press and UCLES 2018

9 Vocabulary 2

Read the instructions. Then do the puzzle in groups of four.

Pair A
Instructions
- Ask and answer questions to find out the missing words in your crossword.

  What's 2 down?   very cold

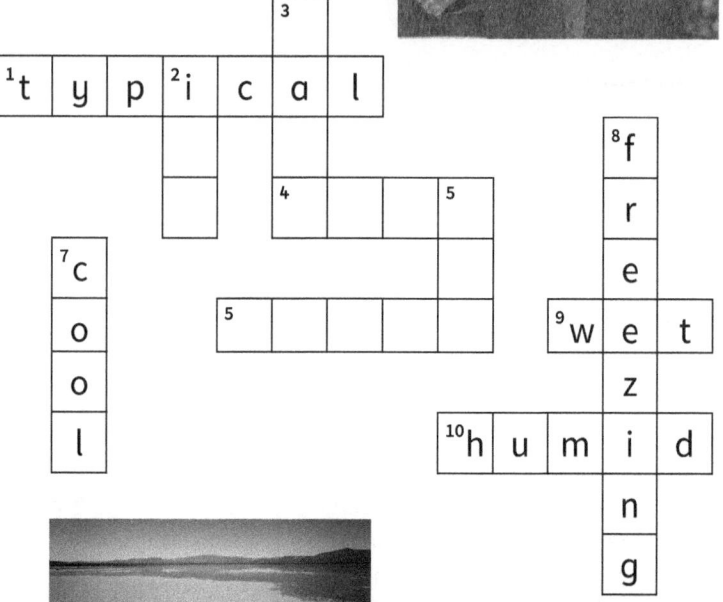

Across: 1 typical, 5 ___, 9 wet, 10 humid
Down: 7 cool, 8 freezing

- - - - - - - - - ✂ -

Pair B
Instructions
- Ask and answer questions to find out the missing words in your crossword.

  What's 1 across?   not unusual

Across: 4 mild, 5 snowy
Down: 3 warm, 2 icy

82   Power Up TRB 6 © Cambridge University Press and UCLES 2018   **PHOTOCOPIABLE**

9 Grammar 2

1 Look at the pictures. Write sentences about what they are thinking with *I wish*.

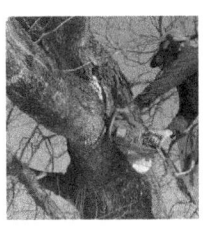

1. _____ 2. _____ 3. _____

4. _____ 5. _____

2 Find and circle the mistakes in the text. Then write the correct sentences below.

The other day I said to my dad, "I wish I don't have to study and work in my life." My dad said that in a way he could understand what I meant, but that learning new things is very interesting and working with others is important. He also thinks that reading boosts your imagination. He wish he had more time to read books. I said, "Well, I wish I could worked only at home. Then I would have more free time."

Then he told me that once he worked with his laptop from home because he had to look after me for a week when I was little, and he felt terribly bored without his colleagues around, even though he argues with them sometimes. Then he added, "Though I wished I have less work and … I'm wishing I was younger…"

_____
_____
_____
_____

3 Think of three wishes. Draw each in the box. Cut out your drawing and swap with your partner. Now guess what your partner's wishes are. Write sentences with *I wish*.

PHOTOCOPIABLE   Power Up TRB 6 © Cambridge University Press and UCLES 2018

9 Skills 1: Listening and speaking

1 🎧 **For each question, choose the correct answer.**

1 What is Shirley's job?
 A journalist
 B singer
 C weather woman

2 What did she study at university?
 A geography
 B science
 C environmental studies

3 What was her first job?
 A banker
 B shop assistant
 C book seller

4 How did she feel about her first assignment?
 A she didn't enjoy it
 B she was happy about it
 C she thought it was boring

5 What was the worst thing about her report from Dorset?
 A the rain
 B the lightning
 C the thunder

6 What is the best ting about Shirley's job?
 A travelling to new places
 B meeting interesting people
 C the variety of the job

2 Work with a partner. Say what you can see in the pictures.

In this picture I can see ...   *I can also see...*

3 Work with a partner. Ask and answer the questions.

1 What is the weather like in your town today?
2 Have you ever experienced extreme cold or hot weather? Where?
3 What is your favourite kind of weather? Why?
4 What outdoor activities do you usually do in the winter? Summer?
5 Why do you think the weather in many countries is changing?
6 What do you think we can do to reduce weather changes around the world?

9 Skills 2: Reading and writing

1 Five sentences have been removed from the article. Choose from the sentences (A–H) the one which fills each gap (1–5). There are three extra sentences which you do not need to use.

The weather around the world

My name is Karin and I live in Iceland. **(1)** _____ This is because of the Gulf Stream which brings warm air from the Caribbean. The average temperature in the capital city of Reykjavik is around 1–2 degrees in the winter and 12 **degrees** in the summer. We never get very hot days in the summer. It is usually **warm, but I wish we had** hotter weather in the summer. Reykjavik is in the south of Iceland. **(2)** _____ Some towns in the north get so much **snowfall** that transport is almost impossible.

I'm Peter and I come from Botswana. Botswana is a country in the south of Africa. **(3)** _____ This makes the weather in Botswana very **dry** and hot. Our summer is from October till March. The average daytime temperature in the summer is 30 degrees and at night the temperature drops by about ten degrees. If you visit Botswana in winter you will feel that the weather is quite **cool**. It is very dry in the winter with a daytime average temperature of 20 degrees and a nighttime temperature that can drop below 6 degrees. I don't like the winter nights because they feel cold. **(4)** _____ It never snows in Botswana, but **I wish I could see snow**!

My name's Chloe and I come from Liverpool. It's a city in the north west of England. The weather in England is usually quite **mild** compared with other countries in the world. We have four seasons. The weather is quite **humid** and we get quite a lot of rain in the spring and summer. We don't have a very hot summer but we do some **sunshine** and, for short periods, the temperature can go up to about 25 degrees. **(5)** _____ We don't often get much snowfall in the winter, but we get a lot of rain and sometimes **gales**! Sometimes **I wish I lived in a hot country**!

A If I lived in a cold country I would miss the hot weather in my country!

B The midnight sun in Iceland happens in the summer when the days are longer.

C The winter is usually quite cold with an average temperature of 6 degrees.

D If you travel further north the temperatures are lower.

E There are a lot of plants in the desert, even though it is very dry.

F We have a large desert in Botswana called the Kalahari Desert.

G Liverpool is near the sea so it's quite windy and humid.

H Most people think it's always freezing in Iceland but that isn't true – it can be quite warm here.

2 Think of the weather in your country. Make notes in your notebook.

1 How many seasons do you have? _____
2 What is the winter like? _____
3 What is the summer like? _____
4 What are the average temperatures in the winter and summer? _____
5 Which is your favourite time of year? Why? _____

PHOTOCOPIABLE Power Up TRB 6 © Cambridge University Press and UCLES 2018

9 Mission Stage 2: A weather forecast

Think of a city or country. Write a weather forecast for your chosen place. Draw a map of the area with weather symbols to show what the weather is like.

LOCAL WEATHER REPORT

Place

Forecast

Map: